Life Gives Me Lemons

Thanks for the support, Silver Fox!

Life Gives Me Lemons

Adventures in Bad Luck and Bold Misfortune

C.J.
9/2013

C.J. Feehan

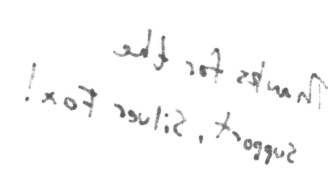

© 2013 C.J. Feehan

www.cjfeehan.com

First published by Dog Ear Publishing
4010 W. 86th Street, Ste H
Indianapolis, IN 46268
www.dogearpublishing.net

dog ear
PUBLISHING

ISBN: 978-1-4575-2338-0

This book is printed on acid-free paper.

Printed in the United States of America

FIRST U.S. EDITION 2013

C.J. Feehan

Life Gives Me Lemons

Born and raised in Randolph, New Jersey, C.J. Feehan is a freelance sportswriter, editor, and media specialist whose articles and photography have appeared in *Ski Racing Magazine*, *The Stowe Reporter*, *S-Media Snowsports Culture*, and on NCAA.com. After completing her undergraduate study at Skidmore College and obtaining a master's degree with a creative writing concentration from Dartmouth College, she resided in California, British Columbia, and New England while she worked as a professional ski coach, a college professor, and a preparatory school humanities teacher. When not busy chasing bylines or snowstorms, she currently lives in Burlington, Vermont, where she happily consumes real maple syrup on a daily basis.

In memory of Dr. Hasse K. Halley (1940-2011)
who always remembered to smile
when life gave her lemons

Contents

CONTENTS

Acknowledgments

This narrative began as a weblog at lifegivesmelemons.com that morphed into a book proposal that was then summarily rejected by nearly every respectable literary agency in the greater United States. My advisor on the proposal, Dr. Hasse K. Halley, was a former bookstore owner and renowned high school English teacher in Vermont, and she believed so earnestly that this book would be printed one day that she insisted we meet in a coffee shop in White River Junction on numerous mornings to discuss my next move in order to secure its publication.

On October 1, 2011, smack in the midst of our planning, Dr. Halley was struck by a car on the road in front of her home and suddenly lost her life at the tender age of sixty-nine years young. The book now you hold in your hands is both dedicated to her and was, in every imaginable way, made possible only by her unrelenting belief in my ability as a writer and in the value of this project as a work of literature.

As for how the manuscript made it from an undesirable book proposal to a published work, I have to thank the sheer generosity of more than three hundred patrons of the arts and fans of my blog who supported a Kickstarter crowdfunding campaign to cover the costs of production. While each pledge was critical to my success, the greatest contributors included: Independent Ski Racing, Sue Fowler and Kevin Holmes, Janice and Jeremy Holmes, the Leek Family, the Masi Family, the Nadler Family, Nili Riemer, the Rolfs Family, the Shiffrin Family, the Warren C. Smith Jr. Family, and Jonathan Lisle Williams.

Without the loving support and financial assistance of my parents, Patricia and Kevin Feehan, I never would have been in a position to get into and then out of so much trouble with that characteristically sly grin on my face. My fearless older brothers Kevin and Michael also paved the way, on several occasions, for me to take the kind of daring, high-flying risks that middle class girls from suburban New Jersey normally avoid. Thanks, guys, for throwing all those shovels and lawn darts and cans of tuna fish at each other instead of at me.

Additionally, I am grateful for the constructively critical support of a select group of close friends whose opinions I respect dearly as well as my editor, Kim Jackson, all of whom proofed multiple drafts of the manuscript to ensure that I wasn't setting myself up for utter failure or a lifetime of embarrassment beyond that which I have already endured.

Finally, to the man for whom I cannot express enough gratitude to match his unconditional love and reinforcement, my life partner and the rock who grounds my soul: Thank you once again, for this and for everything, my dearest Timmy.

My mother wanted us to understand that the tragedies of your life one day have the potential to be comic stories the next.

—Nora Ephron

Preface

Long before these stories ever came close to comprising an entire book, they were just the tales I told to entertain friends at dinner parties or to lighten the mood at social functions. Sometimes I was egged on by a familiar, "Tell them the one about the time you got chased by a bear" or the forever classic, "She ran herself over with her own car, and she'll tell you all about it." If you had to be randomly seated next to someone you had never met before at a mutual friend's wedding, I was the person you wanted to draw.

I came to discover that whenever I told complete strangers these stories about misfortune in my life, they always found them deliriously funny despite the fact that the experiences themselves had been pure misery for me. Some of my yarns, particularly the ones that involve near-death experiences, are downright devastating for my mother to read. Before sharing them on a website for strangers far and wide to find amusement, I first used them to entertain whole crowds in person. But the internet was an easy way to reach a grander audience in a short amount of time.

As the website developed over the course of a year, I worked on framing my narratives into humor that I could share with the world. An unexpected byproduct of this process was the liberation from sadness that I felt as a result, and I learned that I could feel better about the experiences myself by assuming ownership of the stories. So long as I could make people laugh by retelling them, then it made the experiences more valuable to me in the first place. Basically, sucky things suck a lot less when you and other people can laugh about them after the fact.

The day that I came to fully embrace this beautiful life of lemons I have lived was when I practically starting hoping for tragic or nearly unbelievable situations to arise just so I would have more content for my website. It was also at that time that I realized the short vignettes on my blog were destined for something greater than quick reads on the web. The following twenty-one chapters, divided into convenient and concisely packaged tales, are the very best of the best, my collection of the most ridiculous—and in many cases, embarrassing—situations in which I have either accidentally placed or simply found myself.

When I was a young child, my parents were engaged in the kind of nasty and drawn-out divorce that has prevented them from even speaking to one another to this day, almost thirty years later. At family functions, my parents are the ones sitting on complete opposite sides of the room from each other. I firmly believe that what we live through as kids always matters. It can either hold us back, or it can give us superpowers.

After being stationed in Germany as a military policeman with the U.S. Army and then working as a specialist on the floor of the New York Stock Exchange, my father had developed the kind of emotional toughness that was a prerequisite for success in those occupations. He clearly passed this resilience down to his offspring. I have to think that the turmoil my family endured during my early childhood somehow prepared me to be able to laugh after triggering and skiing through an avalanche just as much as it enabled me to break into hysterics after throwing a kayak through my car's windshield.

Despite the dysfunction of an ugly separation, my parents managed to nail the two keys to raising happy children. Regardless of what was going on in their personal lives, my parents repeatedly told each one of their three kids how much they loved us, and they always reinforced through both encouraging words and personal example that we could grow up to be whatever we truly wanted. It wasn't a bluff. My father had three careers in his life and my mother the same. There are no doctors or lawyers in the family, and my parents have been more encouraging of my pseudo-careers as an alpine ski coach and struggling writer than any other two parents in the history of the world.

Aside from my immediate family members whose monikers appear unchanged in the text, all other names in this book are pseudonyms. In some cases, identifying characteristics, dates, and locations have been altered or left intentionally vague for the purpose of quality storytelling and to protect the reputations of those involved. Despite notions to the contrary, I can assure you that I turned out mostly okay, I think, and no friends or family members were harmed (all too severely) in the crafting of this epic narrative.

Have you ever laughed at another person's misfortune? At one time or another, we all have. The Germans even have a word for it: Schadenfreude, which loosely means finding pleasure in another person's misery. When bad things happen in our lives, it can be all too easy to fall into the enticing trap of victimization, a path that rarely leads to resolution. I prefer to take the road less traveled, the thorn strewn path where I tell you all about how much of a fool I have been so we can laugh it out together. Sometimes, life gives me lemons. Now I'm giving them to you.

1
Running the Ladder

The only proper place to start this story is at its very beginning, with my first memory of life. I was five. By many standards, five is considered atypically old at which to process an initial memory, as anyone who fails to recall points in her existence prior to the age of four is thought to suffer from childhood amnesia. But psychologists have also discovered that many early recollections from before the age of three can be unauthentic anyway, and there is an entire field of the profession devoted to false memories. In one particular study, nearly one-third of participants who were exposed to a fake print of themselves at Disneyland later claimed they could recall being there at the time.

I've never been to Disneyland, and there were no faded Polaroids from the day I fell out of the backyard tree house and split my head open. Sure, my parents have retold the story an infinite number of times since that day, but I distinctly remember the sequence of events—like each page in a frame-by-frame action flipbook—that conspired to send blood pouring out of my head and my panicked parents to the doctor. It stands out as a genuine recollection for a number of reasons, not the least of which is the fact that my parents were still together at the time. They would separate that year and eventually divorce, so this and a smattering of other troublesome memories are the only ones I have of my parents while they were still married, quite unhappily, to one another.

My brothers must have asked my father for a tree house, because he suddenly decided to build one for us. Like a lot of really cool dads, my father sometimes made purchases for his children with questionable motives. I'm fairly certain nobody asked for the pool table that showed up in our basement one Christmas morning. He also tried to convince us the next December that we wanted one of those huge trampolines, the professional kind that rival swimming pools in size, both before they were popular and long before they came with any sort of protective netting to prevent young kids like us from killing ourselves while attempting unsupervised double backflips. In that isolated instance, we successfully convinced him not to buy it. Years later, I would acquire one on my own and would spend an entire summer vacation bouncing and flipping on it with a pair of skis attached to my feet. It looked about as ridiculous then as it sounds now.

The tree house was unique. It wasn't the idyllic kind you are no doubt imagining, nestled high between the branches of a healthy white pine. Our tree house was a brown, four-walled particleboard shack that balanced precariously atop the eight-foot tall stump of a dead tree on the outskirts of the woods just behind our home. It sat next to the trailhead of a rock-lined path through the woods that I would eventually build with my neighbor,

Karly, in order to seamlessly connect our yards and for easier access to one another's homes—and the tree house.

In the stifling heat of a suburban New Jersey summer, the tree house doubled as a Vietnam War era sweatbox. In winter, it was an ice fishing shanty that had fallen clear out of the sky and landed perfectly on a stump in our yard, and we hoisted a ladder up so we could access the front door. Despite its visible shortcomings, it served as the hangout for my brothers and their neighborhood gang for a few years before the spider infestation took over and we all outgrew it in one manner or another.

But that very first summer, while the paint was still fresh and all the door and window hinges opened with the smoothness of new hardware, the tree house was really something special. Since I was only five, I wasn't allowed to climb up or down the old utility ladder, painted to perfectly match the tree house while simultaneously making it look less decrepit and dangerous, by myself. I made a point of following my brothers around anytime they went up into it. Looking back, I must have been the most annoying tagalong little sister in history. I would like to take just a moment out of this narrative to formally apologize to my brothers for that, and for always trying to follow you guys around the block on my bike. And sledding on Tammy Hill Trail. Also on that walk in the woods behind the new housing development when we found the construction workers' nudie magazines. The grand adventures to Kroger's to buy vast quantities of candy. I am so sorry; I just wanted to be one of the boys.

I so intently desired my brothers' attention, in fact, that I earnestly believed taking ludicrous risks would impress them. That's how I wound up on the top rung of the tree house ladder convinced that I could quickly run down it like a set of completely vertical stairs. Sure, I could just kick my heels back and make sure I firmly planted a foot on each rung on my way down. I was devising this scheme in my head when my brother Mike shouted, "Hurry up!" because he was tired of waiting for me to descend the ladder, and I wasn't about to give him any reason to doubt that his younger sister was anything shy of the most amazing kid in the whole world. With gusto, I ran down that ladder.

There's this funny thing about ladders, though. Despite the fact that it may appear both feasible and logical to a five-year-old, you cannot actually run down one. I have a friend who once thought he could ride the arc of a ladder as it fell from a roof; as long as he stepped off a rung just before the ladder struck the ground, he reasoned he would be fine. He wasn't. Similar to a former boyfriend who borrowed my skateboard once only to discover that the human body in motion meets quite abruptly with stationary ground, I learned that my plan to run the ladder was rather ill-conceived, but by then it was already too late.

Whoever thought crushed shale was a good landing pad at the base of the tree house ladder also hadn't been struck by sheer brilliance. As I ran down the ladder—I'm pretty sure I made it at least two rungs with nimble grace—I eventually caught my foot and fell forward, effectively catapulting myself headfirst into a pile of razor sharp shale shards. It hurt. A lot. So I frantically ran from the scene of the accident to the sliding back door on our deck as the deepest, reddest blood spurted with each stride from the open wound on top of my head.

I would blame Michael. He would forever bear the burden for telling me to hurry.

My mom acted swiftly with the clarity only mothers who see blood and vomit with regularity can pull off. She grabbed a towel, wrapped it around my head, and began applying pressure. As she escorted me out of the house and into the garage, my father serendipitously pulled his car into the driveway on his way home from work. It was a perfectly timed Feehan family catastrophe. Others, like the day Kevin hurled a spiked metal lawn dart into Mike's neck or when the curtain rod fencing tournament took a turn for the worse, would be less opportune. Both of my parents were available for rescue from my disaster, and my mother held me close against her chest in the backseat of the car while my father drove with all deliberate speed to seek medical assistance.

While speeding in New Jersey is a way of life, it's also a surefire way to go broke by accumulating traffic tickets. My father was not immune to frequent interaction with local law enforcement officials. As he raced his car through town with a bleeding daughter in the backseat, he had the luck of hauling straight through a speed trap. In a frantic voice, he told the officer about my condition. And for the first time in my life, I heard my father not only get out of a speeding ticket but also acquire a police escort to the doctor.

Our family pediatrician was a relic from ages past, the quintessential kind of doctor from a simpler time who might grace a Norman Rockwell painting. His degree from Harvard hung proudly on the wall of his home office while his wife served as both receptionist and nurse of the private practice nestled deep in the countryside of a neighboring town. They were the two kindest people I may have ever met in my life, and no more so on that afternoon when Dr. Knight sewed my head back together.

That handful of stitches and a bottle of Tylenol-Codeine patched me up just fine. As for my second memory, well that was the utter surprise I had when my stitches were finally removed. The procedure didn't hurt at all. For some reason, I figured pulling out the string that held my head together would be painful, but it only tickled a bit. While I wasn't planning to sign up for the ladder running championships anytime in the near future, this revelation opened up a world of possibilities in my mind. The human body was both pliable and easily repaired.

Game on.

2
Santa Claus and the Tooth Fairy

Turning six wasn't a whole lot easier by any means. My birthday came and passed in December as the holidays after my parents' divorce carried a noticeably different tone. It wasn't so much that Thanksgiving and Christmas were any less jolly; they just seemed to highlight the clear schism in our family, especially when it came time to figure out which parent had custody over the kids on any given day.

Christmas, in particular, had forever been my father's least favorite holiday. He's opposed to the commercialism, sure, but I'm half convinced he received coal in his stocking one winter during his youth. Ebenezer Scrooge and my dad would be fast friends during the artificially drawn out block of festivities that drags on annually from November to January. Even though he had long ranted about his hatred for the season, my father still managed to deliver an envious bounty of gifts for his children each and every Christmas morning.

In 1983, when Cabbage Patch Kids made their international debut and graced the cover of *Newsweek*, the dolls flew off shelves. Riots broke out in stores and fights erupted between parents over the must-have Christmas toy of the year. That very same Christmas, as other kids could only dream about getting one of the dolls, I had an original Cabbage Patch Kid waiting for me under the tree from Santa. My father knew the value of the toy and had outbid all the other parents while attending a charity auction. He may have hated Christmas, but he certainly enjoyed making his children happy.

The first winter my parents were apart, my dad still procured a tree (heck, even the Grinch managed to steal one), but it wasn't quite the same as the massive hardwoods that glowed and glistened in our family room in years past. There were the classic decorations and lights and an angel at the top, but the tree felt like it was missing something.

"Didn't we used to have bigger trees?" I asked my brothers as they kicked each other for legroom on the couch while watching *The Dukes of Hazzard*. Roscoe P. Coltrane had just apologized to Boss Hogg for allowing those rascally Duke boys to get away once again. Evading the law or not, I always wanted to be able to jump through a car window like Bo Duke.

"I think it's the same," my brother Kevin replied.

"I guess so," I mumbled to myself before walking through the hallway and down the stairs to the basement.

I loved the basement in our house with its cement floors and brick walls and cold, musty air. In the basement, I could be alone to plot out what I wanted for Christmas. Sears had released its three hundred-page *Wishbook*, a mail order catalog that included every toy I had ever heard of, and some I had not. Mad scientist laboratory kits, E-Z Bake Ovens, and Power Wheels tempted my gaze. I never thought of it as suspicious at the time, but I was required to draw up my Christmas list addressed to Santa Claus exclusively from the toy options available in the most recent Sears *Wishbook*. Each and every year, I struggled to make decisions while paging through Playmobil sets and Play-Doh kits, but I figured Santa was probably trying to rack up some loyalty points on his Sears card.

Christmas Eve arrived sooner than expected, and Kevin, Mike, and I set out a glass of milk and a plate of homemade Nestle Toll House cookies for Santa. In retrospect, the boys had to have been playing along for my benefit at the time since they were already eight and nine. There's a particular age at which one first develops cynicism, and they had certainly reached it by that point. No fat man in a red suit with a furry white collar slides down anybody's chimney with gifts in tow. But the thought that Santa Claus could be any less real than my own two parents hadn't crossed my mind quite yet.

I woke up extra early the following morning, as young children are wont to do on Christmas Day, because I enjoyed staring at the stash of presents before anyone else in the family had a chance to see. Though I knew I wasn't allowed to open any of them until everyone else woke up and came downstairs hours later, I'd try sleep on the couch in the glow of the red tree lights, anxiously guarding the Christmas treasure, waiting while wanting to tear the paper from just one gift to feed my craving. Patience was a virtue I hadn't yet acquired, and time feels like forever when you haven't lived very long.

As I tiptoed downstairs, quiet as could be, the kitchen

clock read 5:47 a.m. It was way too early for anyone else to be awake, but it was late enough to catch a glimpse of Santa's motherload. I walked into the family room, and I was suddenly truck by its starkness. The tree was on the left side of the room, erect and glittering, but the space beneath it, typically reserved for a sprawling pile of boxes, was barren. No oddly wrapped Barbie Corvette or shaved ice machine or Sit 'n Spin. Nary a single present or even a lump of coal. Could children be so bad that they didn't even deserve coal? Santa hadn't even touched the milk or chocolate chip cookies.

The room seemed silent at first, but then I recognized the faint sound of snoring emanating from the other side of the room. My father lay still on the couch, in the same position I had last seen him on Christmas Eve, dead asleep. People had always said my dad looked like someone famous, or maybe just familiar, but even fast asleep on the couch that morning he looked like a polished newscaster. His fine, dirty-blonde hair rested in straight lines just above his ears and swished in an arc across his forehead while his skin, simultaneously rugged and refined, appeared as if it had been through a lot but was always pampered along the way. He did and still does look famous, like people have always told me. But I know he's just my father.

I shook him and shook him and called out his name. No response.

"Dad! Dad! Get up!" I screamed.

"What? Huh?" he asked, awaking in confusion.

"You fell asleep on the couch, and Santa couldn't come. You have to go to bed upstairs," I ordered him.

"Oh, what time is it?" he asked.

"Almost six. What if Santa had to skip our house, and he doesn't come back?" I inquired.

"He'll come back. Don't worry," my dad said, assured that Christmas would go on as scheduled. "You head on upstairs, and I'll be up in a minute."

I thought maybe my father had forgotten about Santa's intricate flight path and the time zones and how lucky all kids are that none of us live in the Arctic poles and how the International Date Line and Judaism make the magic of Christmas possible. Santa had to pass up houses with closed chimney flues. How could my dad be so sure he would come again? I was certain we had missed our chance.

I sulked all the way back upstairs to my room thinking Christmas was done for, that I would have to wait a whole other year for any presents to come. My bedroom door was directly at the top of the stairs, and I didn't hear my father come up even after a few minutes. He had a habit of always falling back asleep even after being woken.

You could shout, "Wake up! You fell asleep!"

And he would predictably respond, "No, I didn't. I'm just resting my eyes." But on Christmas morning when Santa had already missed one delivery, there was no time for anyone resting any eyes. His eyes needed to be in his bed upstairs, not on the couch in the family room.

I walked back downstairs to implore to him to bed once more. But as I neared the landing, I heard the door leading to the garage squeak open. I peeked around the corner of the stairwell to see my father standing tall in the kitchen with a pile of wrapped boxes stacked high in his arms. He made trips back and forth to the family room from the garage, dropping the presents along the way. I snuck back upstairs without any confrontation. I knew. There was no need for explanation.

I was the only kid in first grade with irrefutable evidence that Santa Claus didn't exist. My Jewish friends had called foul on Santa from the very beginning, but every good Christian boy and girl still believed. Now, I too knew the truth. All I could do was hold out hope for the Easter Bunny and the Tooth Fairy.

In a few short months, my faith would be tested. I lost my first tooth in the spring following the worst Christmas ever. It wasn't one of my two front teeth; it was on the bottom row just to the left of the front. I wiggled it with my tongue and fingers for nearly a week, cringing in agony when I caught the nerves with awkward twists. Despite the pain, I turned and pulled and pushed and jerked, but it wouldn't come loose until I finally stopped trying.

"Stop wiggling that tooth," my mom commanded. "The new one will grow in crooked," she portended like someone who had lived through the experience herself. That turned out to be the myth of the century when I grew up to be the only one of her three children who didn't require braces.

That first tooth finally fell out while I ate pudding one day at lunch in the Shongum School cafeteria, though the wiggling certainly expedited the process. I had seen the wonders of the Tooth Fairy in crisp dollar bills that my brothers received from her generosity. Okay, it was a little creepy that a winged creature collected children's teeth, but it seemed like a fair enough trade—supply and demand and all. I had a tooth for sale. It was payday.

My sleep was sound, even with a tooth under my pillow and the promise of a late-night visit from a mythical being. As the morning sky broke through the slats of the blinds and sunlight filled my bedroom, I reached under my pillow and pulled out a single bill that I clenched in my hand. My eyes got wide. My smile got wider. I had never seen such a sight. It was mesmerizing, and I was ecstatic. I ran around the house, from room to room in dizzying circles up the stairs and then back down, waving the bill over my head while shouting, "The Tooth Fairy gave me fifty bucks! The Tooth Fairy gave me fifty bucks!"

As one can probably imagine, my brothers were furious. The going rate for teeth in our household had never exceeded more than a few dollars.

"That's so unfair," Mike reproached. "I've never gotten anywhere near that for a tooth."

Fifty dollars to a six-year-old was like five thousand dollars to an adult in those days. I started to think of all the things I could spend it on: unlimited trips to the ice cream man's truck, a Super Soaker 2000, maybe even a Slip 'n Slide for that slight hill in our front yard.

My father approached me shaking his head, pulled my arm close to his body, forcibly removed the radiant fifty bill from between my fingers, and swiftly replaced it with a five. I had gone from millionaire to pauper in the blink of an eye.

"Sorry, the Tooth Fairy couldn't see in the dark," he said matter-of-factly before walking away, vaporizing my final glimmer of faith in the creatures of childhood fancy.

3
Suicidal Basketball Camp

I f you know of a youth sports camp in the greater New York Metro Area that operated during the nineties, chances are high that I either went to it or considered going to it at some point as a kid. While a chance week-long friendship with Bryant Gumbel's daughter Jillian kept me entertained at the Rutgers Basketball Camp (and provided the only opportunity I've ever had to almost know someone kind of famous), my best friend and fellow tomboy Becky was my usual accomplice at all the others from SoccerPlus to UK Elite to the All-American Soccer Camp.

Becky and I spent the summer months bouncing back and forth from college dorm rooms to practice facilities, oscillating between skill development and scrimmages in basketball and soccer. I'd play pretty much anything at that point; I just loved sports. Even more so, I loved getting away from home in the summer. I never suffered from the common childhood ailment of homesickness. If anything, I had just the opposite. My parents eventually became accustomed to the phone calls from camp when I begged them to enroll me for an extra week or two beyond the date I was originally scheduled to return home. I was the type of kid who wished camp lasted forever.

Although Becky went to a different elementary school on the other side of town, we first became friends at Harbor Hills, a traditional summer day camp close by to where we both grew up, because we were the only two girls in our division who got more excited to be assigned floor hockey as an activity than arts and crafts or cooking. It was the very same summer camp where my brother Kevin and his future wife would realize amidst their courtship that they had attended together in their youth without ever knowing the other person. Photographic evidence later confirmed that they both sang in the camp performance of *South Pacific*, my brother and his wife each serving as the bookends in the standing row of the chorus. Harbor Hills was that kind of magical place.

After meeting Becky there in the summer of third grade, we were practically inseparable. It helped that her father coached youth soccer and basketball in our town, and each season he intentionally drafted me onto his team so Becky and I could play together. We were Building Blocks of Learning for soccer one season and Rec #3 basketball the next. Clearly the basketball league was unimaginative in assigning team names, but I didn't care if it meant I got to play with Becky.

In the summer after sixth grade, Becky asked if I would join her for a week at the Hall of Fame Basketball Camp at Montclair State College, a mid-sized post-secondary institution near our hometown that would subsequently receive the designation of university a few years after our time there. That was the sort of impact we had on the school. But before we even got to camp, there was one caveat to accepting Becky's invitation. Because she had a hectic summer all booked up with other camps, the only week she could attend Hall of Fame was reserved for boys. Only boys. Somehow Becky's father convinced the camp of our superior feminine prowess and maturity, and the camp director agreed to accept us during the boys' session as the only two female participants.

I wasn't actually that good at basketball, but at five foot five I was the tallest girl and nearly the tallest person in my class, and I played center on the girls' town travel team where all I had to do was put my hands in the air to retrieve rebounds. Becky, on the other hand, possessed actual talent, and she was useful in any and every position on the court. Early puberty would eventually catch up with me, and by the winter of seventh grade I became the team's point guard. By eighth grade, I gave up basketball entirely to spend my winters skiing. I had a sneaking suspicion by then that skiing was the sport that would likely pan out better for me in the long run. But in the summer of the Hall of Fame Basketball Camp, I was still taller and endowed with quicker reflexes than most of the boys my age. Even though I had developed breasts before any other girls in my grade and most classmates took to teasing me mercilessly over them at school, none of that ever seemed to come up on the recess basketball court.

The day our camp session started, Becky's parents dropped us off at the dormitory where we would spend the rest of the week. Blanton Hall was aptly named and as bland as it sounds, a concrete structure five stories tall with four wings that extended off a central atrium. There was a dining hall on the ground floor which was convenient at meal times, but the rooms were cinder block bunkers that felt more like prison cells than college housing. Panzer Athletic Center, where the basketball courts were and where we spent the better part of our daytime hours during the camp, was a little over a half-mile walk clear on the other side of campus. For a twelve-year-old who dreaded the timed mile run in gym class, the walk past pretty much every other building at the school to what felt like another town seemed like a military battle trek we had to undertake four times a day.

Despite being the only two girls at the camp, Becky and I made fast friends with two boys in our group, Dylan and Montel. Dylan was a shy, lanky teenager who instantly developed a crush on Becky. Who didn't? Although she was guarded at first, she eventually came to appreciate his flattery. Montel, on the other hand, was a black city kid, a little rougher around the edges, who had a sense of humor to make you laugh your head off all day. His cousin, who lived on a higher floor in Blanton Hall, was a full-time student at the school, so we frequently went to play Nintendo and watch cable television in his room between practice sessions. We were probably breaking pretty much every camp rule by doing so, but we obviously never asked anyone for permission.

We also ordered delivery food every night for dinner. The dining hall, though convenient in location, produced nearly inedible meals. Breakfast was passable because they had a wide assortment of commercially produced cereal options, and lunch was usually sandwiches. But by dinnertime, Becky and I were desperate for pizza and meatball subs and chicken and broccoli. Dylan and Montel had just stopped by when our first Chinese food order arrived, and they laughed as we tried to eat the cold, flavorless meatballs wrapped in dough that were passed off as fried dumplings. Even the takeout was unappetizing. Dylan's interest in Becky was clear by that point, so during an after-dinner game of Truth or Dare, I challenged him to kiss her on the mouth.

Montel and I had to swear on holy heaven that we wouldn't tell a soul about the kiss if Dylan went through with it, which we both did without protest. But as soon as his dry, chapped, awkward teenage lips touched hers, Montel and I were running up and down the floors of Blanton Hall shouting, "Dylan kissed Becky! Dylan kissed Becky!" The atrium served as an acoustic amplifier, and that very same night all four of us were scolded in the camp director's office for being together in a room behind closed doors. Becky was mad at me for playing town crier and getting all of us in trouble, but she forgave me by the next morning as she walked to the gym holding Dylan's hand.

I didn't have a camp boyfriend, but I didn't care too much. I had something much more coveted in the early nineties than teenybopper lust. After determining that my Reebok Pumps could never live up to their marketing hype, I convinced my mom to splurge on a pair of gold and maroon limited edition Air Jordans just in time for basketball camp. The shoes looked and felt supernatural with the golden silhouette of the iconic player slam-dunking on the sole and upper cuff of the high-tops. I loved those shoes so much that I wouldn't even think of wearing them outside. Much like Mr. Rogers, I wore street shoes for the extended walk across campus only to sit down on a bench and change into my Air Jordans once on the court, a ritual that instantly garnered the attention of the high schoolers at the camp who thought I was pretty cool, you know, for a little girl and all. I probably should have been scared or intimidated when they threatened to steal my kicks if only the sneakers were big enough to fit their feet, but instead I felt special.

The Air Jordans served me well over the first day of camp, but by the second day my feet were rubbed raw around the toes and heels. I had picked up the shoes just before coming to camp and, since they were exclusively for indoor use, never had a chance to break them in until I was shuffling around the court and running sprints. By the afternoon of the second day, all my toes and both my heels were a blistered mess. The athletic trainer had to tape up my feet just so I could make the walk back to Blanton Hall that evening.

It was a drizzly morning and the older guys who all worshipped my sneakers were bored of traipsing to the gym by the third day, so they decided to ride the campus shuttle bus instead of walking. I convinced Becky that we should do it too, mostly because my feet were a swollen and painful disaster but also because I relished in the attention from the high schoolers. Dylan and Montel decided to walk, but Becky and I piled into a seat on the shuttle bus. The older boys were pumped that they had figured out a way around the long walk, and we were all sitting pretty high on our horses until we arrived at the gym to a harsh greeting by the camp director.

Although we were never informed that riding the college shuttle bus was in violation of camp policy, apparently it was something we were supposed to know intuitively. The punishment was one that every basketball player has faced numerous times during a career. We stood shoulder-to-shoulder on the baseline for Suicides, a sprint workout that involved running back and forth between every line on the basketball court. If you could complete the task in some absurdly fast time, then you were excused from subsequent rounds, but everyone else has to go on until they either puked or the coach gave up and moved on to another drill. If you didn't beat the buzzer on the very first sprint, all hope was essentially lost because there was absolutely no way to be faster once you went two Suicides deep into the pain cave.

Becky, quite understandably, was furious at me once again for luring her into hot water. I figured we would run our sprints and then laugh it out later like any other petty girl squabble. But as I stood on the line to face our punishment, the athletic trainer called me over to the bench and told the coach I couldn't run because of my blistered feet. Had I run the sprints, I likely would have had to sit out the whole rest of the week of camp. But with the more conservative course of action, my feet healed in two days and I only missed a few drill sessions along with the infamous Suicides.

The high school boys were jealous that I got out of the sprints, but they didn't hold it against me. Remember, I had the Air Jordans. But Becky was so irate that she refused to talk to me for the remainder of the day. We went to sleep in our prison cell without speaking a word to each other. The next morning, we walked to the gym in silence. I was in a camp full of boys and the only other girl, my best friend, wouldn't even acknowledge my existence. Finally, on the walk back to Blanton for lunch that afternoon, Becky broke out into a raging harangue. I tried to defend myself, but Dylan and Montel were keeping score in the verbal spat and they awarded Becky all the points clearly out of favoritism. In a life full of impassioned lecture and debate, I have never lost a verbal spat so convincingly as I did the day I attempted to persuade Becky that I would have run the sprints by her side if only the trainer had allowed.

I earned a state championship title in extemporaneous speech the following year, but one of the older guys who was eavesdropping on our argument even chimed in, "Damn, girl, you got schooled."

Twenty years later, I'm still not sure Becky has ever forgiven me for making her ride the bus and then face reprimand alone, but we went on to play hundreds of soccer and basketball games together throughout our teenage years. I couldn't rewind time to make up for my past blunder, so when she made the varsity soccer team as a rookie freshman, an accomplishment beyond comprehension since the squad went 11-0-2 that season and was named the top-ranked public high school girls' soccer team in the nation, I became her number one fan. Since I was relegated to the freshmen roster, we were no longer on the same team for the first time in our lives. During a varsity Halloween night game under the lights, I ran up and down the sidelines of the field dressed as a soccer ball, handing out candy and cheering my head off for Becky who sat idly on the bench for the duration of the match as a backup goalkeeper, all a part of my lifelong plan to do whatever it takes to make up for those damned Suicides.

4
Roundabout Road Trip

I was the smart ass in class who tested the teacher's
patience but who always made everyone laugh. So by
the eleventh grade when I started to feel entitled to personal days just like the faculty, the people responsible for
my education didn't seem to miss me all that much. Sure,
my math teacher once asked, "What, no snow today?"
when I happened to show up for calculus class on the
morning of the exam review in the middle of winter. But
generally speaking, as long as my grades were excep-
tional in all those Advanced Placement classes, nobody
bothered to care where I was during the school day. I was
also treasurer of the student council, so people trusted
me. I can barely figure out the tip for a restaurant bill and
still count on my fingers, but even then I was quite the
persuasive speaker. The fact that an entire school of more
than sixteen hundred students elected me to manage its
extracurricular budget because I had witty posters and a
clever speech but can't even balance a checkbook is one
of the more convincing reasons why I put very little faith
in politics to this day.

My truancy was a stealth operation camouflaged by
scanned and forged letters from colleges I supposedly visited

and a calculated scheme that cracked the attendance policy at my public high school. It worked like a charm back
then, but I still awake to cold sweats in the middle of the
night brought on by nightmares in which Randolph High
School administrators force me to retake algebra and
chemistry in order to retain every degree I have subsequently obtained. In short, I don't recommend cutting
class nearly as often as I did.

The best day I ever cut class was in the fall of my
senior year. Cold temperatures had blanketed the Northeast just before Thanksgiving, and Hunter Mountain in
upstate New York boasted one of its earliest openings in
years. Two ski friends from other high schools were itch-
ing to get on snow as well, so we devised a plan to cut
class on a Friday and drive to and from Hunter in a single day. It was a two and a half hour ride in each direction, but I possessed the three keys to instantaneous
teenage celebrity: determination, moderate athletic skill,
and a car. Car was the term I loosely applied to the gaso-
line dependent engine and metal frame I cruised around
town in. My brother would later confirm that the three
thousand dollar Honda Accord my dad bought from the
Middle Eastern man who ran a chop shop in Edgewater,
New Jersey was in fact a Frankencar, or two vehicles that
had been in accidents and were welded together to create
a single automobile. The radio and heat never worked, so
I drove around with a battery powered boom box in the
backseat while wearing ski clothes whenever the temperature dropped.

At the early start of the winter, I picked up my
friends Taylor and Dani and headed due north for snowy
Hunter Mountain. Taylor was a total hottie with a wild

default. Some people have a wild side or a wild streak, but wild was Taylor's status quo. In stark contrast, Dani was the tame, reserved good angel who sat on my opposing shoulder. She had recently taken a liking to a mutual friend of ours who was a freshman at Cornell, and on the whole drive up to Hunter we had to hear about Aaron. Aaron, Aaron, Aaron. Conservative Dani would later go on to become a loving mother and wife sans Aaron. Who could have predicted? But even if we had possessed this foreknowledge at that moment, we still would have been unsuccessful in persuading her that Aaron wasn't worth her time.

We envisioned ourselves ripping top to bottom ski runs while our friends sat in biology class and learned about the Krebs cycle. When I pulled into the parking lot at Hunter Mountain, however, our delusions crashed into the stark reality of early season skiing. A white, narrow ribbon of snowy death weaved its way from the peak and came to a crude ending in a muddy bog roughly fifty steps from the chairlift loading area. Patrons stomped over piles of hay with their skis underfoot in order to load the lift. Tickets, of course, were full price. In our haste to ski at the beginning of winter, we had forgotten what a report of "early season conditions" actually meant.

Never one to waste an opportunity, I called for a round two rally and suggested we continue northward nearly four more hours to the Vermont ski mecca of Killington. By a majority rule vote, Dani was forced against her will to join us for the trip extension. I pulled into a gas station in Tannersville, New York to refuel and stock up on snacks, and that's when Taylor first revealed...

"I brought weed," she said as she stuffed a Ziploc bag full of pot into my glove compartment. Taylor would often drop bombs like this when there was absolutely nothing you could do about it. She had a penchant for being screwed up in precisely the kinds of things you didn't really want to be messed up in when you were an honors student applying to top-tier colleges. You know, real innocuous kinds of things, like smuggling drugs across state lines. One time when Taylor ran away from home and was living with her older boyfriend, her mother phoned my house and threatened to send the police over to search my property for her daughter. I called her bluff, and Taylor eventually went home on her own accord. But this was par for the course in our friendship.

"I'm not cool with that," I responded as she laughed it off and ran into the convenience store to buy a drink. Dani sat in the backseat and freaked out for a little while. When Taylor returned to the front passenger seat, she took the final two sips from her Pepsi and then tossed the empty fountain cup right through the open window and into the middle of the parking lot.

"You're going to pick that up, right?" I asked.

"Why?" she fired back.

The first sight I had of the cop who was parked in the bank's lot across the street was in my peripheral vision as I caught a glimpse of him throw on his lights, cross the road, and then pull up alongside my car. There I was, cutting school for the day with two equally underage accomplices and a bag of pot in my glove compartment. This wasn't going exactly as envisioned.

"Someone accidentally dropped her cup, huh?" the officer inquired through his rolled down window.

All I could think was, "Please don't ask for my registration, please don't ask for my registration, please don't ask for my registration." My registration was in the glove box, under Taylor's bag of weed.

"She was just about to get that, officer," I said as I glared at Taylor with eyes of death.

Taylor exhaled, "Oh come on."

"What are you kids doing up here?" the cop began to dig deeper as Taylor exited the car, picked up her cup, and discarded it in the garbage can that was next to the car all along. I remembered I had Jersey plates on the car, and we were in upstate New York.

"Faculty in-service day at our school," I lied. "We're on our way to go skiing."

"You can ski now?" he asked suspiciously.

"Oh, yes, sir," I said. "Hunter just opened, but it isn't very good. So we're on our way up to Killington."

"Have a safe trip," he said, "and try to keep all the contents inside your car from now on, ok?"

"Yes, sir, no problem. Have a good day," I said before closing the window. I scowled at Taylor and ordered her to put on her seatbelt, and then I continued on toward our final destination.

We arrived at Killington just after lunchtime, paid full price for lift tickets, and slid around on manmade snow for three hours. By the time the lifts closed at four, I was exhausted and wondered how I would ever make the drive home to New Jersey. It was, after all, the Dark Ages between the decline and fall of Jolt Cola and the glorious rise of Red Bull.

Dani had what—at the time and without a map for reference—seemed like a pretty good idea. She suggested we stop off at Cornell on our way home from Killington to visit Aaron. We could sleep in his dorm room and tell our parents we were staying at each other's houses. Maybe we had seen it work once in a Stove Top stuffing commercial, so it seemed like a foolproof plan. Dani had an additional stake in the proposal that seemed to swing her down our continued path of delinquency, but it sounded like a reasonable solution with my limited experience navigating New York. In present day with GPS or an iPhone, I could never be persuaded to drive three and a half hours out of the way for someone else's booty call. But this was 1998, and we were still convinced we'd all have flying cars before everyone was driving around with miniature satellite computers on their dashboards.

I became distressed when the road signs to our next major landmark in Aaron's directions began to indicate vaster and vaster expanses. At a critical juncture when we realized our money was running low, we made the group decision to eat only Taco Bell from there on out. We had only our ski clothes and Taylor refused to set foot on a college campus without swankier duds, so during one of our pit stops she came back to the car wearing a completely new outfit.

"Taylor, we're eating Taco Bell to conserve funds and you're running off to buy clothes?" I shouted. "I don't even know how we're going to afford the gas to get home."

She shook her head at me and replied, "Calm down. I stole this outfit from Kmart." Tack one more criminal offense onto the court docket.

Although Aaron was expecting us, he had no warm welcome for anyone other than Dani, and even that greeting was palpably tepid. He took us on a quick jaunt around campus, walked us to a frat party that was promptly broken up by security after someone pulled the fire alarm, and then escorted us back to his cramped and cluttered dorm room. Dani got to share his extra-long twin bed while Taylor and I battled for floor space. It was November in Ithaca, and these Ivy Leaguers had their bedroom window propped wide open; I guess Cornell really is the easiest one to get into. I slept for a total of five minutes that night in between bouts of nearly freezing to death.

The next morning, we bummed some cash off Aaron and walked to my car in the visitor lot where I discovered my entire compact disc collection had been stolen. The Frankencar's windows never fully closed quite right, so it was basically the easiest vehicle ever to break into. I never thought I had anything of much value in it until my Ace of Base and Jewel albums along with the rest of my Columbia House CD collection had vanished into thin air. As we drove off the Cornell campus and through Ithaca, Dani was in an even sourer mood. She kept saying how terrible the whole trip was, Aaron hadn't given her the attention she sought, and he was hardly glad to see her. She repeatedly exclaimed that the whole drive was one colossal waste of time.

Taylor finally lost it. "A waste of time?" she yelled. "At least you got to sleep in a bed last night. We had to rub butts on the floor just to stay warm!"

We drove home mostly silent for almost four hours with no music and hardly a word spoken. As my car puttered into the driveway back home, the gas gauge registering empty, I made a decision that proved invaluable to my crime-free future. I decided that I would still cut any class in school I wanted to, except maybe for geography.

5
Aussie Rules Golf Cart Baseball

I'm not exactly sure how the Australian lifeguards even got hired at the day camp where I worked during long summer vacations from college, but I was certainly happy to have them around. They had funny accents and introduced me to disgusting inedibles like Vegemite and meat pies and scrumptious national treasures like Arnott's Tim Tam biscuits, a delicacy now available in the States from October through March each year courtesy of Pepperidge Farm. Back then, the Australians had to smuggle the cookies into the country for me each summer, which they were more than happy to do. The Aussies had toned bodies, never wore shirts, and frequently sat around in only their Speedos. Even the girl they brought with them the final summer I worked at the camp turned out to be a total rock star and became my lifelong accomplice in misadventure from the Jersey shore to the Great Ocean Highway in Victoria.

Just how hot were the Australian lifeguards? Good looking enough that during our downtime at work, I took half-naked pictures of them in highly suggestive poses. Then I had the photos enlarged, printed in full color, and bound into a calendar, and I sold the finished product to every female member of the camp staff for ten dollars a pop. That's probably criminal these days, but I had quite the unbridled entrepreneurial spirit even back then. The guys considered it complimentary. And they were only quasi-legal summer workers anyway, so what recourse could they have possibly had?

My job at the camp fell into gray area. I had worked on the athletic staff one year and as a counselor another. But the final summer I collected a paycheck from the business, I was assigned to programming. It was my responsibility to organize the logistics of every special event we hosted from Wild West Day to Campus Circus. One afternoon I was buying kegs of sarsaparilla at a liquor store. The next, I was applying for a municipal permit to land a helicopter on our soccer field so a man dressed up as Dumbledore could jump from it to officially declare the opening of Color War. I wasn't exactly a member of the administrative staff, but I used the company credit card on a regular basis, and I was allowed to drive one of the golf carts.

Having access to one of the camp golf carts was like owning a key to the city. It separated supervisors from underlings—the haves from the have-nots—and enabled the driver to transport herself from the central office to the farthest stretches of the high ropes course or the boating pond in the blink of an eye. On those sweltering afternoons when the temperature topped out in the high nineties, a spin around the facilities on the golf cart was the closest you could get to air conditioning. It went beyond privilege; it was the defining characteristic of our summer caste system.

My brothers had both moved in with my father to be closer to their jobs in Manhattan, so that left two entirely empty bedrooms in my mom's house. One of the Australian lifeguards, Hudson, became a permanent resident while a handful of other people seemed to float through the additional spare room as if we were running an international youth hostel: Brits, Aussies, random travelers who somehow knew someone from camp, the professional rugby player, and pretty much every one of Hudson's friends from his semester abroad at Colorado State University. My mom joked about keeping a guest book by the revolving front door. But one night after a deck full of people who were brought together from all parts of the globe by tenuous association joined voices in singing Don McLean's "American Pie," my mom decided it was worth having near strangers stay at the house for a whole summer if only for the purpose of entertainment. Plus, Hudson mowed the lawn every week and helped mulch the front yard bushes, so my mom was pretty cool with it.

I would be lying silly if I claimed that we didn't raise serious hell during that summer of utter debauchery. There are inside jokes from twelve years ago between our gang that can instantly conjure up moments as if they occurred just last week. Along with my closest female colleagues, I established a strict dating code called dibs—the ultimate pecking order that listed which male counterparts we could aim to impress without sacrificing our delicate lady friendships with each other. It failed miserably. Still, we went to parties as a posse and did our best to remain cordial despite the raging jealousy that inevitably develops between young women vying over a limited supply of attractive mates.

Perhaps the highlight of that summer was a weekend of festivities at our friend Brody's house in Connecticut. Brody was tall and dark and gorgeous, with a smile to woo a thousand princesses and the body to back up the charm. Even though he wasn't Australian, he made it into the calendar. We loaded one of the camp vans with a keg of the cheapest beer we could find and landed in Danbury just in time to continue drinking for the next two days. On Saturday night, Brody invited his high school and college friends into the mix, and we played games like shoulders and flip cup well beyond the witching hour. After what I thought was a short walk into the woods to clear my head and perhaps my stomach, I returned to Brody's house to find the entire party shut down and all the doors to the house locked tight.

A moment of panic ensued when I feared being eaten by a bear or dying of exposure while sleeping on the front lawn; instead, I found one of the doors to the camp van miraculously unlocked. It still reeked of that cheap beer, and I endured a cold night's sleep on the bench as I curled myself tight into a ball and shivered for hours under the driver's seat cover hoping to shake myself warm. The next morning when I was hungover and exhausted and on the brink of violent illness, Hudson did his best to intentionally make me throw up.

"Runny eggs! Spoiled milk!" he yelled from the other side of the bathroom door like an annoying older brother. Nobody could believe I was locked out all night, and they insisted at least one of the doors to the house had to have been open all along. And maybe it was, and I was just too drunk at the time to find it, but that didn't change the fact that I slept in the van. While everyone went to see *The Perfect Storm* that afternoon, I rode out a typhoon of nausea on the couch.

But none of this compared to the trouble we caused with the camp golf carts. Brody, Hudson, and a few others had taken one of the rigs for a drive down the road to the local pub after hours one day. When they emerged from the establishment to drive home, they found two police officers suspiciously eyeing the cart. Brody tried to walk by unsuspectingly to scope out the situation, and that's when the cops called him out by name. He had accidentally left his wallet in the golf cart. We'll never know if one of the guys claiming Eagle Scout status got them off the hook that time, but the police took pity and drove them back to camp without ever informing the owner. The guys returned to the pub later with a pickup truck and some two-by-fours to retrieve the cart and return it to camp before anyone ever noticed it was missing.

That should have sidelined the shenanigans for the duration of the summer, but it only seemed to fuel the fire. Because once they got away with a stunt of that caliber, the possibilities were wide open for all of us. So wide open, in fact, that one evening as we polished off cases of Corona in the camp office while wearing assorted costumes from the theater program's dress-up trunk, we became enthralled in an intense game of beer bottle bowling. One competition led to another, and we eventually found ourselves divided into two teams and armed with the full fleet of golf carts on the baseball field under the midnight sky. Like the hazy origins that prove challenging to pin down for so many sports when digging through the archives, Aussie Rules Golf Cart Baseball was more organized than a pickup game but still lacked any official set of guidelines or regulations.

The game proceeded roughly along these terms. A player stepped up to the plate with a whiffle bat in hand and idling golf cart nearby. The pitcher lobbed a tennis ball high into the mysterious shade of night. Assuming any contact was made between the bat and the ball—denoting a probable base hit—the batter then jumped into his golf cart and raced to first base before the field player could tag the cart with the ball. Of course, darkness often concealed the locations of both the struck tennis ball and the bases, but the carts all had headlights to offer the team at bat a slight advantage.

It sounded like a completely reasonable game until you considered having to tag up after a fly ball. We hadn't. Folks in the line up—myself included—were bored waiting to bat, so we decided to ride along as passengers in the speeding carts. As one driver accelerated towards first base after a hit, mine was well on his way to second when we doubled back with haste to tag up. Contact was made all right, but it involved the less than harmonious collision of two golf carts and all aforementioned occupants. After accounting for everyone's body parts and failing to identify any serious injury, we turned to the vehicles. Despite the lack of light, one could still make out the scratches and dents to the front of my cart and the other one flipped on its side.

We never considered how much it might cost to repair the damage, and we certainly didn't consider how lucky we were that no one was hurt. The only thought that crossed our minds was getting fired if we ever got caught. How many drunken Australian lifeguards does it take to pick up a rolled golf cart? Depending on how much lifting each one is willing to do, anywhere between two and four. And how many college-age employees does it take to never mention one word of it to upper management? Every last one of us—including the few who eventually did get fired for subsequent infractions. We all could have been packing our bags at pretty much any moment that summer, but the risk only added excitement to the beauty of those eight reckless weeks we got to spend in each other's company, designing new games that we played like champions.

6

Six Easy Tips For Seducing Your Very Own Canadian Bootfitter

TIP ONE FOR SEDUCING A CANADIAN BOOTFITTER:

Return to your illegal summer job in Canada, the job where you coach skiing without a visa for an American company on the Blackcomb glacier. You'll have to schmooze your way through customs by telling the agent you're going on vacation—for two months. There is no way you are on vacation, but if you say it with the kind of conviction to persuade even yourself, you'll slide right through on your way to the quintessential resort town.

It's a kick-ass gig, the sort of job that when other people hear about it, they won't believe you actually get paid to do it. But then again, you hardly do. The pay is so low that those same people would be much less impressed if they knew the exact value of your compensation for the amount of work you have to do. Actually, they would be appalled, but you'll get a great tan and will come home with tons of stories about skiing in the middle of the summer. So you should definitely go.

The local bootfitting shop sponsors the camp you work for because the owner of the shop has a ski racing daughter who needs to be coached, and Whistler is so much closer to his home than Chile or the French Alps. Plus, they speak English in Whistler, and that's a real bonus. As a part of your job—your somewhat illegal job—you will be sent to the aforementioned store to clarify details regarding the relationship between the camp you work for and the bootfitters. Take note of the guy who manages the shop, the guy you've sort of known for three years but never bothered to pay any attention to because he always seemed geeky before, kind of like a glorified shoe salesman. He isn't geeky anymore. He's ditched the glasses and he's grown a patch of fuzz under his lower lip (and you've recently figured out what that might be good for).

TIP TWO FOR SEDUCING A CANADIAN BOOTFITTER:

Pretend to be flattered by the bootfitter's sophomoric advances and unabashed forwardness. Transform every ski-related service question into carefully crafted innuendo. Leave open-ended messages on his voicemail under the guise of conducting business. When he gets you alone in his shop for the second time, he'll whisper in your ear that he wants to do naughty things to you. Play dumb. But after he buys you a drink whose name you can't pronounce on the outdoor patio of the Hard Rock Cafe and then invites you to his bachelor pad that's decorated like the Polynesian Resort in

Disney World, let him further elaborate on what he had in mind.

TIP THREE FOR SEDUCING A CANADIAN BOOTFITTER:

Agree to run away to the undeveloped property that the bootfitter owns in a remote location off the coast of the Pacific Ocean for a holiday weekend. Canadians don't go on vacation; they go on holiday. Adjust your vocabulary accordingly. Ride the ferry. Take your Subaru off-roading, go skinny-dipping in a mountaintop pond, build a fire during drought season and have the overly cautious lesbian neighbors call you crazy, bound across moss strewn logs in an enchanted forest, and make passionate love for two straight days.

When you get back to Whistler, drop an insane amount of cash on a downhill mountain bike that will be stolen exactly three days later. It will be worth it in the end because the bootfitter will be with you when you discover the cut lock, and you'll collapse to the ground in a puddle of regretful tears. The experience will bring you closer together. You will feel his heart beating while you rest your sorrowful head on his chest. He will hold you tighter than your mom did when you were bleeding in the backseat of your father's speeding car after falling off the tree house ladder when you were five. Try as you might, you will never be able to purge this moment from your memory.

TIP FOUR FOR SEDUCING A CANADIAN BOOTFITTER:

Leave Canada much later than you were supposed to. Go back to California. Change your entire life.

Instead of staying in the city for the year and aspiring to greatness, take a job in the mountains and aspire to make rent each month. Trust me, you won't write any prose of significance for at least seven years anyway. You aren't cut out for law school either, regardless of what your high school teachers might have told you. Who were they kidding? Just reading the logic puzzles on the admissions test makes your brain hurt.

Send the bootfitter a postcard, letter, or package every couple of weeks. Burn him Jack Johnson and Donovan Frankenreiter albums. Sign up for unlimited long distance calls to anywhere in North America. It will be three dollars cheaper if you limit your plan to the continental United States, but you'll probably want to call that bootfitter in Canada every once in a while.

TIP FIVE FOR SEDUCING A CANADIAN BOOTFITTER:

Never refer to this bootfitter as your boyfriend.

TIP SIX FOR SEDUCING A CANADIAN BOOTFITTER:

Carve out a long weekend and fly back to Canada. You're going on a mini vacation for real this time. You don't even remember what a vacation is. Bring your new bike, the bike you couldn't afford the first time around but replaced immediately without considering the financial ramifications when the original was stolen. You'll spend the next two years paying off this impulsive act on your monthly credit card bill. The bike looks just like the stolen one, but it isn't exactly the same. Still, it's your excuse for travel. Even after all the phone calls and care packages, it seems like you might need an excuse to visit that bootfitter.

ONLY ONE TIP FOR LOSING A CANADIAN BOOTFITTER:

Show up to ride your bike after not seeing the bootfitter for nearly two months. He will pick you up curbside at the Vancouver Airport in the sketchy van he recently bought to transport his new dirt bike. The handle to the door will stick and the seatbelt won't work, and you'll pray he doesn't drive off the side of the Sea to Sky Highway on the drive up to Whistler. Expect things to be the same as they were the last time you lay in his bed, when he held you close and tried to comfort you. Lean in to kiss him. He won't kiss you back. He'll tell you he's saving kissing for more romantic encounters, like with a girlfriend.

This is his way of saying you will never be his girlfriend.

Wonder if you even wanted to be his girlfriend in the first place. When you are suitably unable to answer this question for yourself, get out of bed in the middle of the night because you feel cheap, like a prostitute, like Julia Roberts in *Pretty Woman* when she'll do anything to Richard Gere except kiss him on the lips. Not the end of the movie when she's the princess. We're back at the beginning of the film, when she's still a hooker in trashy clothes. You will never be the princess; keep things in perspective.

Sleep on the couch. It will be freezing in the living room, and you'll curl up in a ball and shiver all night. It's a lot like the night you spent on the bench seat in the van parked in front of Brody's house a few summers ago, but it feels like there is more on the line this time. The following morning, get into a disagreement with the boot-fitter over the status of your relationship even as friends, feel tears running down your cheeks for the first time since your bike was stolen, and then watch the bootfitter leave for work before the sun has even risen. Agree to call him, to stay in touch, but don't give your promise a specific timeframe. You'll need more than just a few hours to think through all of this.

Try to sleep in at least until rays of light peak through the window shades. Your eyes will be closed but your mind will be racing. Wake up, climb the ladder to his loft, and turn on the computer to figure out how to get to Vancouver in time for your flight. While checking bus schedules, you'll recognize an envelope you sent him weeks ago, back during Tip Four, tucked into a stack of papers. You know it's wrong to look through those papers, but you're touched that he kept the envelope and not just the letter. You want to know if he saves all of your letters and their corresponding envelopes. He does.

But he also saves all the letters from Lisa and Jill and Courtney and Kelly. They are dated one week ago, three weeks ago, last month, last year. Try your hardest not to throw up, then throw up anyway.

7
Just a Little Avalanche

E verybody makes small though no less embarrassing mistakes in their daily lives that they hope nobody will notice: Spilled coffee in a café, a misstep running up the stairs, or that pile of documents bearing sensitive information blowing in diverting directions clear across a public park. But some mistakes are so massive and equally idiotic that after committing them, you cannot help but be overtaken by the immediate urge to run far, far away to a secluded island for a considerable amount of time. Maybe even forever.

There's no such thing as just a little cancer or just a little sex, and there's certainly no such thing as just a little avalanche. Worldwide, mountainside snow slides claim more than 150 lives annually and cause injury to a number of other individuals who are caught in their destructive paths. Survival stories easily qualify as *60 Minutes*-worthy content even during busy news weeks. They are incomprehensible disasters that call to mind risky mountaineering and skiing exploits.

The unpredictability of snow pack is something I would eventually learn more about while living in Lake Tahoe during one of its winters of near record precipitation. But at the start of this potboiler, I was an inexperienced Easterner who had just moved to California and was still lacking in knowledge of the dangers of unseasonably late snowfall, the likes of which had pummeled the Pacific Northwest in April and May of the year in question. I was also 23-years-old and, therefore, arguably invincible.

I regretfully confess that alongside an equally carefree colleague, I caused an in-bounds avalanche at the Blackcomb Ski Resort in British Columbia, Canada in the summer of 2003, and it was at least ninety-five percent my fault. I've never been very good with numbers, but I feel personally responsible for at least that hefty percentage of accountability. Even better than causing the slide, however, was the fact that nobody even noticed it at the time. I have been publicly ridiculed for dropping a plate of food in a cafeteria, for running myself over with my own car, and for humiliating my friends as well as myself at a charity run. But for causing an avalanche? Not one word. Because until I first wrote about it a few years later, nobody aside from my partner in crime ever knew how the slough pile came to reside at the bottom of the Couloir Extreme that late June afternoon.

When my father read the account for the first time, this was the exact point in the story that he decided he was never going to let me go skiing again or travel outside of the country. These are the kind of verbal restrictions he places on me that I laugh off with frequency. Idle parental threats can be even more patronizing in adulthood; but they show that he cares, and for that I am eternally grateful. It's comforting to know that if I were to perish in an avalanche, at least one person would miss me.

The sudden sliding movement of snow released by natural or human triggers causes avalanches. Basically, if you move around on top of unstable snowpack, it can break away from the surface on which it rests. If this occurs within your vicinity, then you are inevitably headed for an unpleasant, uncontrollable ride of undetermined distance, speed, and consequence. In the spring of 2003, Whistler received an atypically high amount of late-season snowfall after a fairly uneventful winter, so the pack on both Whistler and Blackcomb mountains was not as effectively incorporated into a natural base as it would have been had the precipitation arrived continuously and more gradually throughout the season. A Canadian mountain primed for a slide is the setting for Act One. Enter, skier's left, our wily cast of characters.

The glacier on Blackcomb had just opened for summer skiing. As was the tradition for coaches, at the end of our first day of labor on the hill I asked my coworkers if anyone was interested in skiing out the couloir instead of traversing down the front side of the mountain. Skiing the Couloir Extreme could save us a ride on the T-bar and a circuitous, boring, exhausting trudge through mounds of heavy slush on the Green Line trail. Additionally, we all had to ski while carrying out gear, like water coolers and cordless drills, as well as bags of garbage with us, so the fastest line to the bottom of the mountain was most always preferred.

Of course, the couloir was closed in the summer. There was an elaborate fence in front of its entrance that you had to shimmy under. Yes, there were neon signs posted everywhere warning of imminent danger and possible death should you choose not to heed the directives and ski elsewhere. We could not have been more appropriately warned and encouraged to take a different path. But sometimes the thing you're really not supposed to do becomes precisely the thing you have to do.

It was a thick, soupy day in the clouds where the path to the bottom of the hill was most easily recognized by following dark stationary objects, like lift towers, to their end. We checked off our first day of work on the glacier and prepared for the journey to Whistler Village where we all hoped to be greeted by more cheery weather and possibly a few beers at the Amsterdam Pub. Despite eliciting all three Aristotelian appeals of ethos, pathos, and logos in a most convincing argument, I couldn't rally a quorum to ski the couloir. All of my coworkers chose to ski the significantly longer but safer route down the front side. All of them, that was, except for Brad. Brad was the kind of guy who would slackline between skyscrapers in New York City if you asked him. And he would probably do it while holding a beer, and even while taking the occasional sip.

Brad wasn't exactly a coach, and that was probably a good thing. He was responsible for logistics like making sure all of the equipment was accounted for and we had enough burgers at the weekly barbeque. He carried no fewer than three radios at any given time and always looked lost in thought, or possibly just lost. He talked incessantly about rock climbing and drinking and drinking while rock climbing, but he was a graduate student pursuing a master's degree in business administration. You could tell that Brad had a lot of potential. To do what, exactly, still remained to be seen.

The Couloir Extreme in the summer is a beautiful in-bounds trail that makes you feel like you are as far away from a ski resort boundary as you can get. It can be deceiving because you still know you are right there, in the heart of Blackcomb. But at the end of a long day dealing with kids and all the work associated with ski racing, ripping turns down the Couloir Extreme to the top of the Solar Coaster chairlift was the perfect way to feel as if you had quite possibly the best life in the history of the world. At the bottom of the run on a nice day, you were required to pinch yourself.

It wasn't easy to get under the fence with our skis and water coolers and backpacks, but Brad and I wiggled under the netting undetected in the cover of fog. I made him ski first, but we ended up carving nearly side by side, tight turns at the entrance while dodging the exposed rocks at the narrow, funneled top of the trail. We could hardly see each other, or the rocks, or anything other than the thick fog in front of us. As I smoothly rolled from one set of edges to the next with complete abandon, I felt this indescribable connection to each snowflake beneath my skis. For a moment, I felt absolute flow, the kind of mystical connection sports psychologists devote entire careers to describing, understanding, creating, and then attempting to recreate.

With my sense of sight compromised in the murk, I had reached skiing nirvana. I have experienced a similar feeling on amazing powder days, and still it was nothing quite like this. I was having a moment inside of a moment until I realized, maybe it wasn't exactly flow. I wasn't sensing a mind-body connection between my feet and the snow. In actuality, I was being pulled rapidly down the mountain in heaps of slough up to my waist. I was the snow, and the snow was out of control.

I used all my leg and core strength to cut out to the left side of the trail where rock outcroppings ultimately protected me from the sliding wave of snow. I couldn't see much, but I could hear. Snow doesn't usually make much noise. It's peaceful as it gently falls from the sky to the ground. When it's more frozen and a ski edge cuts over, sometimes there's chattering. But snow sliding in a confined couloir rumbles as deep as thunder.

As the slide passed behind me down the open slope, I called out for Brad. Thankfully, he had used the same instinctive technique to avoid disaster and wasn't far away. We looked at each other and shook our heads in the way you do to say "Oops" without having to say a word. We had made a mistake.

I mumbled, "That might have been the stupidest thing I've ever done." Brad concurred. And then like two moronic lemmings who had somehow been granted a second chance at life, we decided to continue into the valley below the couloir to assess the trail damage from the slide, up close and in person.

Gargantuan boulders of snow as hard as rocks sat at the bottom of the avalanche's path. But if a couloir slides in the middle of a resort and nobody is there to see you trigger it, did it ever really happen? We didn't seem to think so, as Brad and I hiked out of the couloir's basin to the top of the Solar Coaster Express in our sneakers with skis slung over our shoulders and boots dangling from our backpacks. Two short chairlift rides down to the village below proved to be a most clandestine getaway route.

8
Quarter Century Birthday Blowout

As a born and bred Easterner, it came as a slight surprise to my family when I finished graduate school and promptly forded rivers west to carve out my destiny on that final frontier of California. Luckily, I didn't die of dysentery on my journey across the Oregon Trail, nor was any buffalo hunting required for survival. Aside from being dumbstruck at the Golden State's department of motor vehicles agency where no official proof of residency was required to obtain a driver's license, everything else about California was as I expected. The sunshine was warm, the homeless were aggressive, and days at the beaches of Santa Cruz were predictably cloudy.

I had settled in the East Bay and was looking for work in San Francisco when someone walking along the sidewalk at the end of my block in Oakland was targeted in a drive-by shooting. While I was fairly certain the attack was gang-related and my life as an innocent bystander wasn't directly at risk, the scare ultimately proved to be justification enough for another move. I

wasn't looking for a new neighborhood; I was looking
for a new way of life. Nearly two hundred miles due
northeast was Lake Tahoe, the Shangri-la of skiing, and
the lure of the mountains was too convincing to ignore.
My second cousin twice removed on my mother's side
was a detective in nearby Reno, and it was nice to know
that if I moved to Lake Tahoe I would have a relative
close by who could watch out for my safety.

With all my worldly possessions packed tight in the
car once again, I drove out of the city and straight into
the welcoming arms of Mother Nature. I had already persuaded the expat British headmaster of a boarding school
for competitive winter sport athletes to hire me as an
English teacher and coach, but I still needed to find an
apartment. In a local coffee shop owned by a former
Olympian, I browsed through printed newspaper classi-
fied ads like someone who had never heard of Craigslist.
The sunlight reflected through the window, shining down
on a perfect property. After I convinced the Bay Area
family who had posted the advertisement that I was gain-
fully employed and a trustworthy tenant, I emptied my
car's contents into the one bedroom in-law apartment on
the ground floor of their Donner Lake vacation home.

Things were lining up almost too perfectly with my
dream job scored and coveted accommodations landed in
one of America's greatest destination resort towns. It was
sunny every single day and the crystal blue sky served as
a picturesque backdrop while everyone anxiously
awaited the arrival of winter. I had been warned that it
snowed a lot in Tahoe. What people failed to mention
was that the storms wouldn't be forecast in inches like

back East. If it's going to snow in Tahoe, you can count on multiple feet falling from on high.

Winter suddenly blew open the door, and what had been a warm and dry, browning landscape was swiftly replaced with blankets of frosted white. I was used to a more gradual changing of the seasons, but the mountains of California were as abrupt as two Buckingham Palace guards trading off shifts. A day after riding my bike in what was disguised as the weather of late summer, I was slinging skis over my shoulder and bounding to the chair-lift.

My first day of coaching coincided with the morning following both my twenty-fifth birthday and a mandatory social function hosted by my employer's board of trustees. Despite a few carefree summers, I had never partied much in college or graduate school and had missed out on my roaring early twenties while I worked for two years as a Doogie Howser-like college professor. I was, in most cases, the very same age as the vast majority of my students at that time. In order to compensate, I acted twice as old during the precise years in my life when I should have let loose. I was a super nerd. Having reached my twenty-fifth birthday thousands of miles removed from that past life, I felt I was finally entitled to a full-fledged celebration to mark the occasion. It was time to let out the sails, at least a little bit.

Though it's more ideal when your closest group of pals organizes a birthday party on your behalf, I was living in the center of Bro-brahville and not on an episode of "Friends," so any festivities that took place in my honor were going to require self-planning. I figured if all my coworkers were roped into the board of trustees' dinner that night anyway, then asking them to join me downtown for a few birthday brews afterward would likely receive a warm reception. I designed a clever Evite and implored my new colleagues to come celebrate at the Quarter Century Birthday Bash. Positive responses rolled in, and I looked forward to my first birthday party since my Sweet Sixteen almost a decade earlier.

The board of trustees' dinner was meant to be a nonevent that night, simply a function we needed to endure out of obligation before heading to a local watering hole for a couple drinks and then off to bed. But the president of the board found out it was my birthday, and he announced as much to the entire crowd during his opening remarks. From that moment onward, it seemed as if every member of the board made it his and her sole mission that night to get me as lit as possible on multiple glasses of red wine.

Before making a complete fool of myself in the company of the board, I slipped away from the dinner and hitched a ride downtown with our designated driver who insisted I take a birthday swig from his glove compartment flask. The taste of unidentifiable but foul hard liquor hung on my breath as we descended the switchbacks to the valley below. By the time I walked into the Bar of America in the heart of Truckee to begin celebrating my birthday, I should have already been on my way to bed.

Friends and colleagues purchased congratulatory drink upon drink for me until my head swirled into oblivion. Everything was blurry except for when a fellow teacher at the school began lecturing me in the bathroom.

"Chris-tine Fee-han, you are in a public restroom! Get your face off the toilet seat!" she commanded. I was well beyond control at that point and once I finished heaving, my peers had to escort me from the bar with my arms draped over two sets of shoulders. I realize this is a position all too common for sorority girls, but I had never been in it before in my entire life. Friends gave me a ride home to sleep it off and demonstrated enough concern to leave a bucket at my bedside. Even in this state of complete disarray, my punctuality at work the following morning was never in doubt. I still managed to set my alarm clock for seven, a few minutes before the time I would need to leave for my ski coaching job at the mountain.

Getting up in time for work was tough but by no means impossible. It was a scheduled meet and greet morning and I wouldn't have to coach the following day, so I reasoned I could pull it off. After all, it was just a few hours. I drove to the mountain the first Saturday in December with all my windows down, and the cool air felt therapeutic blowing against my face. I was pretty sure I had dodged a major bullet, but I still stopped at a convenience store on the way to the resort to stock up on Gatorade that would be necessary to survive a full day of skiing with kids. When I waltzed into the coaches' meeting appearing more alive than I should have been, the same people who intentionally got me bombed the night before looked like they had seen a ghost.

"I can't believe you're here," they all said in hushed voices. "You were a mess last night."

"A job is a job," I replied before finding a seat in the ski team office. As the meeting proceeded, the collective body heat in the room created a discomforting stuffiness in the air. I started to feel less like a pro and more like someone who desperately needed a bathroom. The moment my boss was finished explaining the plan for the day, I had the sudden urge to get out of the building. I ran out of the room past a steady stream of parents unloading their children for the first day of skiing, exited the front door, and proceeded to round the backside of the clubhouse where I then began to projectile vomit the telltale hangover combination of water and artificially dyed electrolytes. Rehydration would have to wait a few more hours.

After chewing a piece of gum, I greeted my athletes and their parents (some of whom were the very same members of the board who had forced me to binge drink wine the previous evening) with a jovial smile on my face despite the fact that my head felt like a cinder block atop my shoulders. I called my athletes to group up, and we rode the chairlift to the top of the mountain. The first day was all about unstructured play, freeskiing, and the kids getting to know each other, so we were in one massive group with a handful of coaches working together to supervise the bunch. As can often be the case in these situations, we were overstaffed for the job at hand. Since the other coaches had pegged me for dead anyway, they stationed me at the top of the lift for the morning while they skied laps with the kids. I didn't have the energy to actually ski, but standing around on skis was totally manageable.

I checked in with each athlete at the top of the run over the course of a few hours before deciding to rehydrate again. A short walk off trail and behind a tree provided cover, but the small sips of Gatorade came back up as quickly as they went down. Without an ounce of fluid in my system, I started to develop a world-class dehydration migraine, and there was no way I could keep up the front much longer. Just before lunch, I called my boss to tell him that for my own sake as well as that of the kids, I had to go home. There was plenty of coverage on the hill, and I wasn't serving a critical function anyway. He agreed and sent me on my way without much discussion.

It took me until that night to be able to hold down water. I spent the entirety of the day shivering in bed, chilled to the core in the fetal position. Not that I even wanted to, but I couldn't eat for two more days. It became evident over the next forty-eight hours that I had developed an acute case of alcohol poisoning as a direct result of the Quarter Century Birthday Bash. Once I rebounded from my deathbed, my boss called me into his office for an unexpected though deserved stern talking to where he threatened to fire me if I gave him one more reason to do so. I would ultimately spend the rest of the winter as a Prohibition era teetotaler because I had every intention of keeping my job, but I was still struggling to find the right words for a proper apology during the reprimand.

"I know the reputation of your program was at stake as a result of my irresponsible behavior, so I want to apologize for having to leave the hill early the other day," I heard the words creep out of my mouth with utter shame. He was one of the people who had bought me birthday drinks at the bar and then laughed at my severely impaired state of mind.

"I'm not going to tell you to never do it again," he said as his mood softened and his tone took a turn for the didactic, "but learn how to pound a beer in the morning, kid. You'll be much better off that way."

9

Wind River Blisterness

Despite living in the adult version of Disney World, I grew ever restless in the summer months while killing time between Tahoe ski seasons. There were only so many lazy mornings sipping coffee, afternoon bike rides up the pass, or entire days spent lounging on the shores of the lake that I could bear. Although I was teaching during the academic year, it felt like ages since I had finished graduate school and the nagging itch to learn something new tugged at my skin. Leisure time for an adventurist can be both a blessing and a curse, liberating and maddening all at once.

As a young girl, I watched my older brothers, Kevin and Mike, explore the vastness of the natural world and build miniature wooden racecars with the Boy Scouts of America. I rode to Mount Allamuchy with my mom to pick them up after a week of Boy Scout camp one summer, and on the ride home they amused us with tales of shooting BB guns, learning to pitch tents, sailing, and honing their skills as archers. I was a Girl Scout, and all we did was peddle cookies door-to-door that we didn't even bake ourselves in order to fund an organization that encouraged us to collect downright comical patches, like the social butterfly badge, to sew onto the world's ugliest vest. The same week my troop made dream catchers out of yarn and twigs, my brothers went on an overnight canoe trip where they had to carry all of their gear and food in packs while porting the boats around shallow river beds. The Boy Scouts were busy being tough while the Girl Scouts were being sold a false sense of accomplishment.

The one time I did get to go camping with the Girl Scouts, we slept on cots in permanent platform tents that required no pitching. The most taxing part of the experience was carrying our sleeping bags the few steps from the parking lot to our massive canvas sleeping structure.

"Everyone is responsible for carrying her own stuff!" our troop mom announced as we took ten muddy paces from her minivan's trunk to the tent's wooden front door that swung open on a hinge. We ate dinner in a dining hall but then toasted marshmallows over a controlled fire pit, thus earning our camping badges without learning a damned thing about camping.

The worst part about being barred at birth from ever becoming a Boy Scout was that I was predestined to live a life where learning how to fight off bears would prove leagues more useful than knowing how to hunt for clothing sales while comparison shopping. I was born to be a Boy Scout, but gender had dictated otherwise. By the end of middle school, I called bullshit on the Girl Scouts and settled into the protected life of a suburban teenager while waiting out nearly a decade before the call of the wild would lure me back.

In what felt like the outdoorsy capital of the contiguous United States, I wore plenty of Patagonia but was still lacking in precisely the kind of skills I would have acquired as a kid if I had been the third son born to my parents. Instead, I was only prepared to paint pre-made pottery and check into a hotel. At my new California home, I had started rock climbing on Donner Summit after work with friends and was enthralled by the challenge of planning my route up weathered granite as opposed to using artificial holds at an indoor gym, which had been my limited previous experience with the sport. With a summer of free time to fill and the desire to learn more about self-sufficient camping and rock climbing, I signed up for a multi-week course with the National Outdoor Leadership School (NOLS) based in Lander, Wyoming.

My specific course was the school's original offering, a mountain range backpacking clinic that included instruction on navigation, rock climbing, and fly-fishing in the Wind River Range of Wyoming. I was finally going to learn everything I never did as a Girl Scout but should have, even if I had to wait until my mid-twenties to do so. In the weeks leading up to the trip, I hunted for deals on camping equipment at Sierra Trading Post and gathered together the recommended packing list contents like a champ. I hiked up Donner Summit in my brand new Merrell boots to break them in for the miles upon miles of bushwhacking I was promised in the brochure, and I did everything within my power to prepare myself for the journey ahead.

I was as ready as ready could be. But the night before I left to drive the twelve-hour route to Lander, where my course was set to start, I happened to catch a

Dr. Scholl's commercial for gel shoe inserts during the last television show I would watch for a month. A woman wearing the most uncomfortable looking high heels danced along sidewalks like she was in running sneakers, and I thought about the fifty miles of hiking through the brush of Wyoming in my stiff, high-topped boots that lay ahead. In a last-minute decision, I grabbed my custom orthotic insoles for skiing and slid them into my hiking boots before shoving off.

If I had learned anything from my Air Jordan experience at basketball camp a little more than ten years prior, I would have known not to change anything about my shoe setup just before embarking on a multi-week hiking trip. But my orthotics had been constructed especially for the contours of my feet and my feet alone, so I mistakenly assumed they would make for a more pleasant hiking experience out in the Winds.

After loading up our fifty pound backpacks and riding in a bus to a trailhead in the middle of the middle of nowhere, we started walking the route that would guide us over mountain passes and around some of the most beautiful lakes I had ever seen. Our course instructors had warned us all about blisters. We were likely to get them, but if we were proactive in treating hot spots as they developed in our boots, we had a good chance of nipping them in the bud. For the first few days, we were encouraged to take frequent breaks and use moleskin to protect the most sensitive areas on our feet.

The first hours of our initial day in the wilderness were giddy, and we exchanged stories about our past experiences in nature. I processed basic details of the other participants, two women and nine guys, including a doctor, a few fellow educators, and some recent college graduates. By the afternoon of that first day, my feet started to hurt around the outsides of my pinky toes on each foot. During one of our breaks, I asked for the blister kit and went to work taping my toes and around my heels to prevent friction at those tender points.

When we reached our camping site, I had to change into my sneakers before I could even help pitch the tent. I was assigned to share a tent with the other two ladies on the trip, also twenty-something teachers who wished the Girl Scouts had imparted more practical abilities upon them. My pinky toes were red and puffy and my heels were beginning to rub raw, so after setting up camp I walked to the nearby lake to find respite by soaking my feet in the icy bath.

Upon waking the second morning, I discovered classic blisters all over my toes. The swollen skin was filled with fluid, and I drained them as best I could without compromising the protective skin over the rawest parts. After wrapping them in more moleskin, I joined the group for our trudge to the next campsite. I have always been strong willed and the type of person who finishes what she starts, but my pain threshold was waning with each step. The adjustable hiking poles I had packed became crutches, and I bore my full body weight on just my wrists. Each member of the group helped lighten my pack by carrying some of its contents until what was on my back was practically an empty fabric shell. That night, our instructor finally took a look at my feet.

"Those are the worst blisters I have ever seen," she said with the kind of seriousness a doctor would use to inform a patient of a malignant diagnosis. "If those don't get much better soon, we're going to have to evac you."

Evac was the abbreviation for evacuation, and that was her way of telling me that my toes looked bad enough that she was concerned about infection. Since we were in the middle of the middle of nowhere and had to hike as a group each day to arrive at check points and our final destination on schedule, any illness, injury, or infection required that a course participant suffering an ailment be removed from the wilderness via ambulance or helicopter to avoid slowing down the whole group.

The last thing I wanted was to be kicked off the course for swollen toes, so I became intently focused on—if not obsessed with—managing my blister situation. My goal for the course shifted from learning all kinds of new skills to basic survival. Although I had sensitive feet, these blisters seemed unusually severe considering that I had sufficiently broken in my boots before the trip. Something seemed amiss about my boots as I sat with my feet in another cold lake hoping not to attract flesh-eating bacteria to my open wounds. I had to figure out why I had the worst blisters my NOLS course instructor had ever seen in her life.

"Eureka!" I thought as I walked back to the campsite in my untied sneakers that had to be opened as loosely as possible to handle my blistered appendages. The only variable in the whole equation was my orthotics. Could the custom designed insoles actually be the cause of all my pain and suffering?

A close examination of my boots revealed a small gap between the custom orthotics and the outside edge of my foot, a dangerous chasm into which the tips of my pinky toes had likely fallen. My hiking boots could not have been better suited to manufacture blisters than they were with those custom footbeds inside. But knowledge was only half the battle in finding a cure, as I was hundreds of miles from the nearest Payless ShoeSource with no useable insoles for my boots. I tried walking in them without any layer between my foot and the boot sole, but the rough interior surface only further irritated my already mangled toes. As the threat of evacuation loomed if my feet didn't heal, I was desperate to find a viable solution.

I thought to myself, "What would MacGyver do?" But there was no readily available answer since I wasn't trying to escape capture or make anything blow up. Still, I was running out of time and needed a fix. While pondering the best natural material from which to fashion new footbeds, I overheard the doctor in our group engaged in intense conversation with the instructor.

"I don't know how much time we have, but I know we have to get him out of here immediately," the doctor said. Their mannerisms let on that something was seriously wrong, but since I was a she and not a "him," it couldn't have anything to do with me.

Josh, another one of the participants in our group, had pulled a fishhook from his finger a little under a week earlier after miscasting a fly rod, and he woke up that morning with pain and swelling in his hand and noticeable discomfort everywhere else. By early afternoon, he was sweating profusely and had muscle aches. The doctor suspected tetanus, and the potential that this life-threatening disease was the root of these bizarre symptoms was confirmed when Josh confessed that his immunizations were not as entirely up-to-date as they should have been. He had a friend with a medical license sign off on his health form for the trip without any examination or review of his records.

I was granted a stay of execution when the whole group had to rally around getting Josh the medical attention he required. Suddenly, my blisters were a distant concern. An evac team was mobilized with the task of hiking Josh out to the nearest trailhead for rescue. Since my feet were as swollen as the Stay Puft Marshmallow Man, I was given three days to rest with the remainder of our group while we awaited the return of the evac team, minus Josh. By the second day of the encampment, I realized I could use my knife to cut the insoles from my sneakers to fit perfectly in my boots. Giving up my sneaker insoles was a sacrifice worth making in order to complete the full curriculum of the course.

It turned out that Josh had a nasty bacterial infection but no tetanus, and I survived until the very end of the course with only moderate soreness in my feet. I didn't know how to thank Josh for creating the ultimate diversion that enabled me to finish out the trip, but I was happy to give him the book I had packed so he could read something in the hospital. And though I knew he didn't intentionally risk life and limb on my behalf, he did happen to save mine. Plus, I had another copy of *On the Road* waiting for me at home if only I could withstand the twelve-hour drive back once I finally took my last step of the course.

10
Cut the Rope

C ontrary to popular belief, there is such a thing as too much snow even for a skier, and it fell in Lake Tahoe over the week of Christmas during the last winter I lived there. Three feet blanketed the town of Truckee each day for three days straight until all the roads in and out of town became impassable, and the ski resorts were forced to close because employees couldn't shovel out the lifts fast enough, not that the patrons could get there anyway.

I lived at the base of the mountain and probably would have had to resort to cannibalism of my neighbors like the famed Donner Party had the family whose house I rented not left their entire week's worth of food when they abandoned town before the start of the storm. Over the course of the four-day blizzard, all the gas stations ran dry and the grocery stores were emptied out, their shelves left as barren as a shop at the conclusion of a going out of business sale. With no delivery trucks able to make it to town, supplies ran short and restaurants closed. Vacationers extended their hotel and condominium reservations indefinitely, filling rooms that the guests next scheduled to arrive would never get to see.

While the snow slowed down after Christmas, it never fully abated. Residents of the area dug tunnels from their driveways to access front doors, and everyone was running out of options for where to direct the chutes on their snow blowers. How much snow was there? I went sledding off the roof of my friend's house, and there was hardly a gap between the gutter and the landing. The best ski jump in town was at the bottom of my two-story deck stairs.

When it's a big snow year and you live in a resort town, your family will suddenly have a change of heart and support your decision to move all the way to California if they are permitted to come for a visit. By Presidents' Day, I was rearranging furniture and trying to figure out how to accommodate four fully-grown adults in my one-bedroom apartment. My father, brother Kevin, and Kevin's long-term girlfriend who had never skied before, were Tahoe-bound for a week of vacation.

Though it was a tight squeeze, I found space for everyone with Kevin and his girlfriend in my bedroom and my father and me on the separate trundle bed mattresses out in the living room. We would all share a single bathroom for five days and four nights, but it was a small sacrifice in order to introduce the family to my home away from home.

It had become the sort of winter where major snowstorms coincided with the holidays, and Presidents' Week was no exception. Shortly after my family's arrival, a blizzard settled into the region and drew enough moisture from the lake to keep the system bearing down on the area and producing snow for days. My father had become a fair-weather skier by this point in his life, and he came to Tahoe with the preconceived notion that our powder in California was inferior to the blower of the Rockies.

"You know what they call this snow? Sierra cement. That's right, Sierra cement!" he would repeat all week as if to degrade its quality before even taking a single ski run.

As snow fell steadily outside and my family settled into their accommodations, we all hunkered down in the apartment and watched the cheesy Chris O'Donnell climbing movie *Vertical Limit*. In the opening sequence, a father, son, and daughter are traversing a cliff base when some novice climbers above them lose their grips and compromise the safety of the family. As the three of them dangle precariously from a single rope that cannot hold all of their weights, the father orders his son to cut him free, accepting certain death for himself in order to save his children. In the movie, it seems as if the sister will never forgive her brother for acquiescing to their father's demand.

I wondered what I would do if placed in a similar position. Could I cut the rope if called upon? Would I ever forgive my brother for doing so if he had? The movie hit a little too close to home as we all snuggled side by side seeking mindless nighttime entertainment. Somehow Chris O'Donnell's overdramatic portrayal of a climber had managed to tug at my heartstrings.

My family had come to Lake Tahoe to ski (and my brother's girlfriend to sit in the lodge and maybe learn how to wedge down the bunny hill by week's end), but it was a challenge and a half trying to motivate them to head to the mountain the following day in the middle of a storm that already dropped several feet of snow in my driveway. I did my best to project enthusiasm with the hopes that it was contagious. After a relaxing morning of breakfast and coffee, I finally rallied the troops for a day at the mountain.

Nobody should learn to ski in a blizzard, so my brother's girlfriend stayed in the lodge while we headed out to the chairlift. My father was wearing the most hideous looking pair of goggles ever manufactured, the Bollé Alien, and he looked more ready for a trip to the moon than a day of skiing. I offered him a wide selection of other goggle choices at my apartment before we departed for the mountain, but he obstinately refused. Despite my ridicule to no end, he maintained that the oversized, wrap-around lens was the technology of the future even though the goggles were several seasons old.

"You wouldn't believe the peripheral vision out of these things," he professed.

"You're supposed to replace your goggles every few winters because the glue breaks down and their integrity gets compromised," I replied, hoping he would use one of my other pairs that were far less embarrassing, especially for me.

"I would buy a new pair, but they don't make these anymore," he responded, enunciating his stubbornness in every syllable. The goggles of the future, no longer produced. It was already shaping up to be a priceless day.

After cashing in my complimentary passes to get free lift tickets for my family, we plodded through more than two feet of snow at the base area of Sugar Bowl on our way to the top of Mt. Judah. The wind was howling so forcefully that we could hardly communicate on the chairlift without using hand signals. The only thing I could make out was my dad complaining about how miserable it was outside.

"Terrible!" he yelled. "Sierra cement!" We hadn't even started skiing yet. As we slid down the ramp at the top of the chairlift, my father and brother huddled in close.

"Where are we going?" they asked.

We had started at the beginner area of the resort, and I intended to ski them over to Mt. Lincoln, the more advanced section of the mountain, but it was difficult to see through the pounding snow and following me might not be an option. Despite being painfully slow on skis as a child, sometime between the days my father and brothers used to stand at the bottom of trails hollering at me to hurry up and when I eventually moved to Tahoe, I had developed into the most accomplished skier in the family. I wasn't going to make the kind of cautious turns they most likely would on our way to the Mt. Lincoln quad, so I offered directions.

"Just stay as far left as possible until you see a chairlift, ski past it, and we'll group up in the line for the second lift you see," I directed before pushing off through the powder.

I schussed my way down the Pioneer Trail, cut over to Christmas Tree Lane, and stopped at the bottom of the Mt. Lincoln Express. It was a run I could ski blindfolded and sometimes practically did while carrying bundles of racing equipment. I knew I would be the first one down, so I stayed off to the side of the lift line and waited for the guys.

I waited, and then I waited some more.

Kevin finally came walking over with his skis on his shoulder. He had stopped at the first lift, was confused by my directions, but eventually knew to meet me at the second one. There was no sign of our father.

We waited, and then we waited some more.

A well-known saying in the ski industry is that there are no friends on a powder day, but we debated if that adage also applied to family members. There were limits to my patience, especially when the snow was almost knee-deep. Kevin and I had been waiting for more than ten minutes when I finally made the critical call.

"I'm cutting the rope," I said. "He either got lost on his way here or he gave up and is sitting in the lodge. Either way, he's on his own." Kevin agreed, and we went up to the top of Mt. Lincoln to take some runs together without our dad.

My brother Kevin, the Eagle Scout, once survived a summer of backpacking the high mountain deserts of the Philmont Ranch in Arizona where base camp was 7,240 feet above sea level. He had also run the New York City Marathon—twice. We typically vacationed as a family in Vail, Colorado, and the village's elevation there is higher than the tallest summit at Sugar Bowl. Still, Kevin was short of breath and exhausted after only two runs.

"I don't have any more in me," he said just as I was starting to warm up. It wasn't the most devastating news because I secretly harbored some sense of concern for my dad at that point. While I assumed he was fine on his own, I also knew that skiing was a dangerous sport, and he could have very easily been injured if he accidentally took a fall while trying to catch up to us on that first run.

"That's fine, Kev, because I want to check on dad anyway," I responded, and we made our way back over to the Judah Lodge where we also had left his girlfriend. As we walked in the front door, we found the two abandoned souls sitting together at a table drinking coffees. I was relieved that my father was fine, but I was also consumed by annoyance over his selfish disappearance during a powder day.

"What the hell happened to you? We waited for like fifteen minutes!" I exclaimed.

"My goggles got fogged on the inside, and I couldn't see a damn thing," he replied, "and I was so mad that I threw them in the woods. Then I really couldn't see. Who can even ski in this Sierra cement? I barely made it back to the lodge. How come you didn't come check on me sooner?" he continued.

"I cut the rope," I replied.

"Cut the rope?" he inquired quizzically, "like in the movie?" He seemed offended.

"Exactly like that. Does this mean you're done for the day?" I asked.

"I guess I would consider going back out if you had another pair of goggles I could use, since mine are gone for good now," he admitted.

My two spare pairs of goggles, both of which I had offered him that same morning, were now fifteen minutes away from the lodge back at my apartment. The ski day was officially over after my family blew through two lift ticket comps to take a combined total of two and a half runs at a destination resort on a day most skiers would kill for.

We had never been all that hardcore of a bunch to begin with, but the vision of my father hurling his foggy goggles deep into the trees on the side of the trail confirmed that I had drifted further from my roots than previously suspected. That was the afternoon I had to give up a powder day to play tour guide through the boutiques of downtown Truckee, but I swore it would also be my last.

11
Cult Town Shuffle

Island Pond is a village of 850 residents in the North-east Kingdom of Vermont that most infamously serves as the home of the Twelve Tribes, a religious cult whose property was controversially raided in 1984 by state police and social workers suspecting child abuse among members of the group. No evidence of lawlessness was discovered even after the raid, but to this day the Twelve Tribes community holds an eerie grip over many businesses in the surrounding area. Buy a pair of Carhartt pants at Simon the Tanner Outfitter, and you're unknowingly supporting the cult.

I once accidentally patronized the cult-owned coffee shop while passing through town, and it felt like I had the lead role in an episode of *The Twilight Zone*. The shop had run out of coffee, but its pale-skinned and hollow-eyed keepers were pushing maté and religious pamphlets in its place. As a child of the nineties, I associated all cult activity with explosive fireballs in Waco, Texas and mass suicide pacts involving poisoned Kool-Aid. None of this was reason enough to deter me from inviting a number of my new coworkers to participate in a five-mile charity run in Island Pond, Vermont after I moved back to the area that fall. I thought it would be, at worst, a culturally enlightening group activity to kick off the school year.

One of my coworkers had grown up in the somewhat isolated town, but she had never been in the cult. The rest of us were athletes who could not turn down a fun run twenty-five minutes from home, because in Vermont a twenty-five minute drive is considered nearby. I had recently prided myself on participating in as many community events as possible because those were the only times I was confronted with hard evidence that there were more people than cows inhabiting the Northeastern corner of the state. The cows may have had more teeth than the people, but it was still refreshing to interact with my own kind. Dragging my coworkers along as backup ensured at least the semblance of safety in numbers.

The designated event was the Pond-A-Thon Fun Run to benefit the Taini Mae Kinney Memorial Scholarship, a fund that enabled underprivileged members of the Northeast Kingdom community to pursue higher education. Since we all worked in education, it seemed like a more than noble cause. We drove up in a van that prominently displayed our school's logo, and we had six representatives participating in the run and bike. I was especially excited for the event because I had planned it as a bonding experience for my two new roommates, Beth and Sarah, who were both avid runners. They spent as much time jogging on dirt roads and trails as I did sitting on the couch watching reruns of *The Real World*.

That's not to say I was never a runner. One of my dearest friends from childhood, Julie, managed the San

Francisco Marathon for a number of years. One summer she needed a reliable volunteer to oversee free t-shirt distribution for the entrants, so I offered my services. You would be surprised how many volunteers steal t-shirts, especially t-shirts from a major sporting event like a marathon, and it was one of the ways the organization lost money every year. In exchange for my vigilance in preventing seemingly goodhearted people from thieving all the shirts, Julie offered me a complimentary entry in the race. There was no way in hell I could train for a marathon in the few weeks between agreeing to help and the day of the event, but I figured I could finish at least one half of the course. I was too lazy to wake up early, so the second half route that crossed the actual marathon finish line was my run of choice.

I had run 5ks with no training and could pull off five miles without feeling sore the next day. Two weeks before the San Francisco Marathon, I managed an eight-mile run and figured that was good enough. Thirteen miles wasn't much more than eight, or was it? On marathon day, after manning the t-shirt station like a determined CIA operative, I plodded my 13.1-mile journey of pain from the starting gun to the finish line and then promptly decided I would never run any farther than that ever again unless my life was in jeopardy. I had no idea what kind of person could run the whole thing.

Maybe I had some idea. As previously recalled, my brother had finished the New York City Marathon twice, and I also witnessed the husband of another dear childhood friend finish the entire San Francisco route with absolutely no training. He registered with every intention of preparing but then fell short on time with work and life commitments. Instead of bailing on the whole event, he figured he could at least run the first half. But once he crossed that marker, he felt fine so he just kept running like Forrest Gump. My friend and I tracked his progress online via the chip on his sneaker, and we had planned to meet up with him at the halfway point. When we couldn't locate him, we returned to the tracking website to hunt him down. His wife surmised, "I think he's trying to run the whole thing." And there he was, marked at each subsequent checkpoint all the way to the end. A track star in high school, he jogged with a confident stride across the finish line. His first words after running twice the distance he had intended were, "I need a beer."

The charity run back in Vermont was of little consequence compared to San Francisco, but I was disappointed that the route was advertised as fast and flat when it was nothing of the sort. After I summited the third major incline on course, I was ready to quit in protest. Sarah and Beth, the marathon runners, completely buried my time, but they were kind enough to lap back on course and cheer me through the finish. After all participants were done, the organizers invited us to survey the prize table before the start of a raffle. Everyone who completed the course was eligible for a prize, and a picnic table displayed a hodgepodge of donated goods: Homemade apple pies, freshly picked corn-on-the-cob, golf umbrellas, gift certificates, cherry tomatoes. Somewhere in the mix was a framed picture of a ballerina, and my colleagues and I couldn't decide if the prize was merely the frame with a stock photo inside meant to be replaced with your own, or if the picture itself was intended to hold some value. We joked, in audible sarcasm, that it was clearly the best prize on the entire table.

By the time my number was drawn in the raffle, everything edible had been claimed and there was nothing else I genuinely desired. My choice came down to a plant (which I was guaranteed to kill out of neglect), an umbrella, or the ballerina. I didn't need any of them. Although I had no use for it, I figured it would make for a good laugh, so I grabbed the picture frame.

Holding the ballerina high overhead, I began to do my personal victory dance, a disturbing cross between an Irish Jig and the Running Man with some Sprinkler thrown in for entertainment's sake. I waved the picture back and forth with sweeping arm movements while shouting, "I got the ballerina! I got the ballerina!" as I kicked my heels all the way back to my coworkers. We were in absolute hysterics, nearly falling to the ground in laughter. I teased that we could hang it on the wall in the office of the director of development at the school to help rake in extra donations. "Once they see this picture on the wall, they'll be writing checks out of pity!" I pronounced.

Then an older woman, the kind of soft-spoken lady who could have played bridge with my grandmother before her passing, gently tapped me on the shoulder. As I turned around, she held out a jug of maple syrup and asked if I would consider trading prizes with her. She clearly wanted the ballerina very badly. I hesitated to make the exchange; while pure maple syrup is akin to liquid gold in Vermont, I much preferred the humor inherent in the prize I had selected. And I was befuddled as to why she hadn't selected the picture in the first place instead of the syrup if that's what she wanted all along. In the time it took me to formulate a coherent response, she timidly added, "because that's actually a picture of the woman who this race memorializes."

Not a prize. Not a frame. Not a nameless ballerina or a ridiculous stock picture, but the poor girl who died tragically at a young age in a car accident whose name was lent to this charitable event—this charitable event held in a town dominated by a cult. Have you ever wished you could freeze time like Evie from the terrible eighties show *Out of this World* so you could run away before anyone had a chance to notice how much of an idiot you are? This is a much more necessary technological advance than anything we can discover by sending shuttles to outer space. I'm not suggesting we divert funding from cancer research, but time freezing would have proved ego saving that day. To say that my mortified cohort and I left two lines of tread from the van tires in the parking lot of the Island Pond boat launch as we peeled out with all deliberate speed would be an understatement. It's a miracle anyone still goes anywhere with me.

12
Jay Peak Hike Fest

Back when I worked as a full-time alpine ski coach for almost a living, race days began at 5:15 in the morning as I crawled out of bed already late and then scrambled in the chaos of darkness to get ready. The vans weren't technically supposed to pull out until six, but the head coach (my boss) always left early. Even when I wasn't exactly sure where I was going, he would still leave without me. If it was particularly cold outside, minus ten Fahrenheit like it frequently was before those warming sunrises in the Northeast Kingdom of Vermont, the vans could take a while to clean off and turn over and then a solid twenty minutes to defrost, plus I had to tack on a few more minutes for the walk from my dormitory apartment to the parking lot. Time all added up on those mornings when I was already behind schedule from moment I awoke.

If I was extra lucky, the heavens above would puke ice on my van all night long and leave solid frozen slabs on the windshield as a good morning surprise. On those days, I appreciated that the high school kids I coached were courteous and polite. I realize it seems like I'm being sarcastic, but I'm not. They were the kind of kids who would help you carry groceries clear across campus or load recyclables into the back of a truck for proper disposal assuming you asked nicely. The kids would babysit the children of some staff members for a small fee and would help split and stack wood if you promised them ice cream. They could also be manipulated into competing at otherwise unappealing daily chores when a title of any kind was on the line. I handed out gratuitous World Cup points for windshield de-icing almost every race morning to the athlete who enthusiastically volunteered to chip away at the Arctic circle on the van with our half-functional scraper while I pressured the gas pedal and revved the engine to expedite the melting. The points were supposed to go toward an overall championship that I never remembered to calculate.

My van was the crappiest vehicle in the fleet. It was in and out of the mechanic's shop all winter, and when I inherited it the radio no longer worked. I was convinced beyond a doubt that I was specifically assigned this van because I was my boss's least favorite employee. That's not to say he didn't like me or respect the job I did; he just had twelve other more favorite employees that ranked higher than me. I tried not to take it personally, but I also counted my blessings every time the van made it home in one piece after a long drive.

My van reminded me so much of my very first Frankencar, the one that slowly disintegrated over three years of ownership, that I almost didn't realize how junky it was until the kids who had to ride with me started to get bummed out over drawing the short straw. I liked to think I was pretty cool and provided reasonable entertainment, more so than the coaches who insisted on listening to National Public Radio broadcasts, but the kids were choosing the boring vans over mine. I started getting stuck with the odd ones out or the slowpokes, not exactly my first round draft picks.

In addition to the radio going, I discovered on one particular morning that the cigarette lighters had also broken, so that ruled out using an iPod as an alternative source of music. In a frantic rush, I grabbed a pair of battery operated portable speakers from one of the kids and plugged in an MP3 player for the hour plus drive to Jay Peak. I was at the mercy of the musical genre of choice among teenagers at the time—offensive rap.

With the snow subsiding and the moon beginning to set, I drove straight up Route 91 towards Canada. The moon cast a brilliant orange glow as it peaked out from behind a series of mountaintops along the drive. Everyone in my van was dead asleep within ten minutes of driving except for Dave who rode shotgun. Dave was a quiet, focused, intensely serious young man. I caught him staring out the window at the moon for several minutes before I exclaimed, "Would you look at that thing? Isn't it beautiful?" After some deep reflection and an awkward silence, he finally replied, "Yep." That's the most candid statement Dave would say to me all year.

I kept myself awake on the drive by playing leapfrog with the other coaches, jockeying for pole position as the lead rig in our caravan. My boss was incredibly competitive and always wanted to arrive at our destination first, hence the need to always leave earlier than scheduled. One time on a drive to Sunday River,

Maine, he was the last van to pull out of the parking lot and got stuck behind all the other coaches on a single-lane road winding through New Hampshire. He eventually got the chance to make his move in a passing zone, but he didn't have enough space to get around Kelsey's van in time, and he had to settle into the second spot for the remainder of the drive. He seemed destined to lose the race for once. As we entered a small town and a school speed zone, a passing police officer threw a U-turn in his patrol call and pulled up behind all of our vans before driving by. For the first time in her life, Kelsey was the one who got pulled over. She was let off with a warning, but being detained by the cop for even those few minutes enabled our boss to cruise into the parking lot at Sunday River ahead of all the other coaches. The gauntlet had been thrown for a season-long battle.

Despite the overnight icing on my van, a perfectly dry highway failed to suggest any sign of the inclement weather that struck the area the previous evening. We were heading to a slalom race at Jay Peak, a mountain so close to Canada that you can practically sneeze on the country from the top of the resort's tram line, and it was as bone-chilling and dismal as pretty much every other race morning that January or any January in the Northeast. Slalom is an event that goes off come hell or high water, come blizzard or subzero temperatures. While speed races and giant slalom can be weather dependent, snowfall or wind won't hinder athletes contesting a slalom race, so the forecast was easily overlooked on these days.

As I rolled into the Jay Peak parking lot, not in first place, the mountain was concealed in a thick cloud that draped heavy and damp all the way down to the base area. On our walk towards the lodge, the rumors were already spreading among the coaches and athletes who had beaten us to Jay. Ice on the chairlifts. They weren't running. We were going to have to wait it out until the operations staff could deice the lifts. It's a good thing I'm almost as good at playing cards as I am at coaching ski racing.

The ice wouldn't melt. We played poker and hearts for an hour while we awaited word of any progress. I was cheating and still losing to fourteen-year-olds. We ate breakfast sandwiches and then played cards for another hour. I lost even more hands. In exchange for buying my way back into the game, I had to agree to let one of the kids use the staff washer and dryer in my apartment. As I passed time flipping cards and other coaches drank their fourth, fifth, and sixth cups of coffee, we were butting up against the edge of opportunity. If the lifts didn't open pretty soon, there wouldn't be enough time left in the day to even hold the race. When a quorum of adults was convened to discuss the options, somehow I was invited into the conversation.

Everyone was ready to call it a day, pack it in, and get a seventh cup of coffee for the road. It was going to be a long winter of mornings just like this one, and a cancelled race usually evoked a welcomed sigh of relief. But before we could even exhale, my boss, the one who always left early and who had to arrive first and who gave me the crappy van, proposed an idea: Who needs the lifts? Why not just hike the hill? It would be unfortunate to lose a whole race just because the chairlifts were frozen solid.

Although a slightly unconventional suggestion given the age of the athletes, walking up the mountain for a ski race wasn't entirely unheard of. In fact, slalom races used to require that competing athletes walk up the course before a race, a method known as inspection by ascension. Modern slalom skiers are pretty much wimps compared to the legends of yore who always hiked up the mountain before racing back down it. I had already envisioned a relaxing afternoon sprawled out on the couch in my living room with the television remote firmly in hand when I was forced to abandon that fantasy and set out on foot to hike up the course.

Despite the cold and frozen mist falling from the sky, the walk wasn't half bad. I had gotten into the nasty habit of eating too many pastries before parking my lazy butt on the side of a race trail all winter long, and it was refreshing to start off the day with a physical endeavor. The athletes who had to hike and then race, however, were not exactly embracing the experience as an opportunity for a quality pre-race warm-up. It didn't help that the local racers from the Jay Peak Ski Club were whisked to the start on snowmobiles while the rest of us trudged uphill with skis on our shoulders. I channeled my inner drill sergeant to repeat the plan that got me through that blistery month-long NOLS course in the Wind River Range in order to encourage my ambulatory army on our march: Put one foot in front of the other, troops. Then repeat. Eventually, we'll be at the top.

Results from the race proved to be less extraordinary than the experience itself. After hiking the hill like the Tenth Mountain Division and sweating up a storm, the coaches had to stand out in the cold while athlete after athlete tackled a frozen, crusty slalom course with little tact or grace. We could see exhaustion in the body movements of the kids, and some of the athletes flat out gave up on the first run to avoid having to hike back up to the start for a second run. I couldn't blame them. It turned out to be one of the longest, coldest days in my ski racing career, and likely remains the same for those now-grown kids. But for a few hours, it seemed like my boss' suggestion to hike had been worthwhile. We saved the race even if it didn't bring out the very best skiing, and everyone got to toughen up a bit, except for those who hitched snowmobile rides.

What the Jay Peak Hike Fest of 2008 managed to augment, however, was the already weakened immune systems of all who attended. For the next few weeks, viruses and bacterial infections encircled our school's campus, crippling staff and athletes alike in a festering swarm of illness. A stomach bug turned to influenza and unrelenting coughs developed into bronchitis. I know it's considered an old wives' tale and getting a chill doesn't necessarily lead to catching a cold, but I'm steadfast in my conclusion that race or no race, we all would have been much better off if we just played cards.

13
Sticking It Out

I was enjoying our weekly fish dinner in the school's dining hall just a few days before my departure for a two-week camp in Austria with the men's ski team, and I was nervous about being the only woman in a group of twenty-five guys traveling through Europe. The head coach at the time, Ford, was a well-respected man of deep Christian faith, and he had worked at the school for so many years that he seemed to have a story for every occasion. In a Southern drawl diluted by a few too many years spent north of the Mason-Dixon Line, he captivated the table with memories of previous ski trips gone bad.

"There was that rookie coach we took with us one year," Ford started, "and when we went to pick up the rental vans, he told us he couldn't drive a stick. Can you believe that? Couldn't drive a stick!" The guys at the table shook their heads in disbelief and chuckled.

"Do you need to drive a stick in Europe?" I asked timorously, my voice barely rising over the background noise in the hall. The table fell silent.

"All the rentals over there are manuals," responded Ford. "But you know how to drive a stick, right?" he asked rhetorically.

"Well," I replied, "not exactly."

Ford just so happened to be in the middle of teaching his oldest daughter how to operate their family car's manual transmission, so he invited me out for lessons the next evening. I jumped in the car with him, his wife Susan, and their eldest daughter, Kate, and we went out to practice our neophytic shifting skills in the empty ski area parking lot. Kate was up first, but she struggled to keep the directions straight: Foot on the brake, turn on the car, engage the clutch, release the foot brake, shift into first, trade off pressure from the clutch onto the gas. She repeatedly stalled after shifting into first, and her parents began to lose their patience.

"You're not concentrating," Susan told her. "You have to focus."

"I can't do it!" Kate shouted and then broke down into tears. She tried a few more times with no success.

"This is ridiculous," Susan concluded. "You'll never learn with that attitude," and then she proceeded to walk home up the dirt road. Driving lessons were over before I even sat in the driver's seat.

"Do you wanna have a try?" Ford asked me.

"I think I'm good," I said, and he drove us—minus his wife who was huffing up the hill on foot—back to campus.

The following morning over breakfast, I told the other coaches that the only thing I had learned the previous evening was that Kate might not ever get a license if that's the only car she could drive. Our Slovakian coach

Zdravko overhead me talking about the failed manual lesson and offered his services.

"I teach you to drive," he said in the same autocratic tone he used to wish you good luck or to thank you for doing him a favor. Everything Zdravko said was a command. After lunch, I met him by the school's rusted out green utility truck that was used primarily for property maintenance. He sat in the passenger seat and called out orders, and I was terrified of not following his every directive. But I was having the hardest time shifting into gear.

"Green truck is bitch," barked Zdravko. "If you drive her, you will drive anything," he assured me. He got behind the wheel to see why I was having so much difficulty.

"God damn, no first gear," he asserted before promising, "I will teach you in Munich." He coached the women's team, and they would be splitting off in a totally different direction from the airport.

"You are smart. You will figure out," Zdravko said awfully convincingly. Thus, I was on my own to learn on the rental car while navigating through the bustling streets of a foreign city.

My introduction to driving a manual didn't turn out as harshly as anticipated. Another coach on our trip who knew how to operate a stick was too young to be listed as the driver of a rental vehicle, but I rode in the passenger seat while he transported us the three hours from Munich Airport to our lodging at the Stubacher Hof in Uttendorf, Austria. We planned to ski on the glacier at Kitzsteinhorn, a twenty-minute drive from our hotel through a couple roundabouts and up a few switchbacks. The drive didn't bother me though because I was still able to ride along as a passenger, and I had shirked the need for any skill in driving a manual transmission. The camp was going along quite smoothly until the younger coach who couldn't legally rent a car backed our van out of its spot in the parking lot and struck another vehicle. It was a close call and there was no damage, but our rookie was banned from driving for the rest of the trip.

So much for just being along for the ride. I got behind the wheel and listened to the teenage boys I was traveling with coach me through the driving process. They told me which pedals to press, when to shift, what gear to shift into, when to accelerate, when to brake, and how to downshift as we descended the mountain. It wasn't too bad so long as someone was constantly telling me what I needed to do in any given situation.

The next morning I drove issue-free all the way to the mountain, doing my best to cruise slowly into round-abouts so I would never have to stop, and I made it all the way to the turn into the resort parking lot without any help. As I navigated the van into the uphill entrance, a child carrying skis darted in front of my car, and I had to hit the brakes hard. I had done exactly what I was trying to avoid. I had stopped on a hill.

I listened to everything the boys told me to do, but I couldn't get the van to budge without stalling. Over and over again, just when I thought I had it in first gear, the engine would putter to a grinding halt. Impetuous Europeans eager to get to the mountain at all costs laid on their horns and then blew by simultaneously on the left and right sides of my van while my guys in the backseats ducked down hoping not to be recognized. On one of the attempts, somewhere between efforts thirty and thirty-five, the van finally engaged in gear, and I was able to drive up the short slope to a parking spot. The boys vowed never to ride with me again, but they didn't have much choice.

On our day off in Salzburg, the male coaches were clearly lost and could not find our hotel. Naturally, none of them would stop to ask for directions. We zipped up and down the old town streets and all around the city center, using our radios from the mountain to communicate with each other. Ford kept chattering about turning left on Steinhauserstraße and then right on Mitterhofstraße. I was cruising down Breitenfelderstraße at the time, and I couldn't figure out for the life of me why all the streets in Salzburg ended in straße, because it was so incredibly confusing. Couldn't they think of anything else to call their roads for greater differentiation? Then it struck me like a hard fist to the face: Straße is the German word for street.

We finally located our unremarkable pension at the end of an alleyway, and I walked inside to settle in for the night. As the only female on the trip, I was lucky enough to score my own room everywhere we stayed, but it usually amounted to the smallest space imaginable with the world's tiniest bed inside. Our lodging in Salzburg was no different, and I walked up three flights of stairs and down a long hallway. I turned my key and opened the door to reveal what may have been a room at one time but what was clearly being used as a storage closet. There was no bed, just a sink in a room that was full of boxes and linens. Convinced the male coaches were playing a joke on me, I walked confidently to the front desk where Ford was still sorting out details. Dealing with the stick was headache enough, and I didn't need these wise guys also giving me crap.

"Good one!" I exclaimed. "You really got me. Now, can I have the key to my room?" I requested. Ford looked at me dumbfounded.

"I don't know what you're talking about," he said.

"My room is a storage closet," I proclaimed.

"All the rooms in Europe are like that," he replied, mistakenly thinking I was lodging a hyperbolized complaint about my room.

"No," I countered. "My room is literally a storage closet. There's no bed and the whole thing is full of boxes." He couldn't have planned the prank any better, and he and the other coaches in the lobby were snickering. Then the woman behind the front desk asked which room number I was assigned.

"Oh no, two-zero-one *is* a closet. I am very sorry," she said before handing me a new key to an actual room.

On our way back into the mountains after the city excursion, one of the boys made it his goal to teach me hill starts in the parking lot of a gas station. He was calm and patient and gave great advice. I finally felt like I was beginning to figure out the stick, just in time for our second week of training in Europe.

The next morning, we drove to the ski area while it was still pitch dark out. It felt like the middle of the night as I steered the van into the mostly empty lot to find a parking space. As I rounded a corner and drove down the lane, I suddenly saw something appear in the headlights as they shone down on the pavement before me. I couldn't stop fast enough to avoid driving into the ghostly objects. The front tires hopped up and over the artificial speed bumps with a "thud, thud" as the sound of snapping plastic and foreign swears filled the air.

I had run right over an Italian team's entire stock of skis for the day. The athletes and coaches alike were screaming and gesticulating with aggression, but what kind of idiots lay their skis down in the middle of a dark parking lot? I accelerated through the lane and found a spot far on the other side before I could be firmly identified. The day was already off to a magnificent start.

That same afternoon, one of our athletes fell and injured his thumb, and the appendage immediately swelled to an egregious size. I had to give Trevor a ride to the hospital (amusingly called the "krankenhaus" in German) in the nearby town of Zell Am See. One of the other athletes was returning from injury and couldn't ski that day anyway, so he decided to join us for the adventure. Trevor and Tom hopped in my van, and we headed off seeking medical assistance.

It was hard to find street parking around the hospital in Zell Am See, but the town was full of underground paid garages, so I ditched the van in one of those. We tried to stay entertained in the waiting area of the emergency room, and I gave Trevor specific instructions when dealing with the doctor.

"Let him examine your hand and take X-rays and all, but don't agree to any kind of treatment until I can talk with him," I commanded. Trevor was finally called into one of the examination rooms. About a half hour later he came back out.

"The doctor wants to talk to you," he said, and I followed him into the room. As I entered, the doctor gazed up from his pile of charts and surveyed me from head to toe.

"Ah, zee girlfriend," he said in heavily accented English while giving Trevor a thumbs up.

"No," I replied definitively.

"Zee sister?" he asked almost abashedly.

"No," I affirmed, "zee ski coach." He proceeded to tell me that Trevor hadn't broken any bones, thankfully, but he had torn a ligament in his hand that required immediate surgery. I called Trevor's parents back in New Jersey who agreed that the last thing any of us wanted was surgery in Austria.

"Just wrap it up in a splint. We'll fix it when we get home," I told the attending nurse. A week later back home, a hand specialist would confirm that Trevor had shattered his thumb into several pieces but had not suffered any ligament damage.

All wrapped up and ready to roll, Trevor and I grabbed Tom from the waiting room, and we walked to the van. I backed out of the parking spot and drove up the ramp to exit the garage, but I had to stop just before the crest in the pavement to pay for our few hours of parking. I dropped some Euros into the machine, the gate opened, and I shifted into first to demonstrate my newly acquired hill start skills. Instant fail. The van stalled three times, and the gate in front of us lowered back to its original position. I shelled more Euros out of my pocket and fed them into the machine, the gate opened, and I started the process all over again to the very same end.

After I paid for parking the third time and still couldn't get the van to start, a line began to form behind us at the exit. More impatient drivers honked and shouted, but they also blocked the way for me to back up. I was trapped with no way to drive forward and no chance to reverse. The boys were embarrassed beyond belief.

"Do you want me to get us out of this?" Tom asked. He was a fifteen-year-old, unlicensed kid from Wisconsin, but I figured he had been driving tractors since birth.

"Yes," I exhaled through welling tears, "just get us out of here." We quickly swapped seats by running around the outside of the van. Tom tossed more coins into the slot, seamlessly shifted into first, and drove us through the gate of hell. He turned into the street, rounded the next corner, and then pulled off to the side of the road.

"I guess you'll want to take over now?" he inquired while shrugging his shoulders.

"That's probably the best idea," I acknowledged. We switched seats once again, and I finished the drive back to Uttendorf. As I parked the van in the refreshingly level lot at the Stubacher Hof, I turned around to face the boys.

"Our secret?" I asked, hoping they would oblige. The last thing I needed was to lose my job over allowing a pubescent athlete to drive my rental car in Austria.

"Sure," they responded in near unison, "our secret."

14
Two-Wheeled Dog Chase

U nless you are an entire professional cycling team reading this book en masse, I almost certainly own more bikes than you do. All of my sundry two-wheeled machines, put together, are worth more than my car. I'm that person who usually has bikes galore dangling off various surfaces of my vehicle, and I'm frequently driving somewhere to attempt to ride them in circles faster than everybody else.

I race bikes.

The first bike I paid for myself was a mountain bike I picked up during my freshman year of college, and the next year I added a road bike to the collection. A few years later, I replaced my standard hardtail mountain bike with one exclusively for riding cross-country and another specifically for going downhill. That's right. The bike can only go down hills, not up them. If you try to ride it up a hill, it makes your lungs burn with the fury of a thousand fires and your legs feel so miserable that they want to fall off, and all of this occurs before a voice of reason resounds in your mind, "This one is your downhill mountain bike, fool! Ride it in the other direction!"

Three bikes could never be enough, because in the autumn there are these funny races where you ride what sort of looks like a road bike in gnarly off-road conditions, through sand and mud and over barriers and down stairs, and this insane sport invented by Belgians requires its own special kind of ride, the cyclocross bike. So naturally, I have one of those, too. And though I could run errands around town on any one of my other four bikes, I wouldn't look as cool as I do on my faux vintage cruiser.

Of all the bikes, it's the cruiser that garners the most public attention. By far the cheapest of the bunch, my cruiser is designed to look like a bike from the fifties. It glistens and sparkles, and riding it through any downtown district will undoubtedly draw clever remarks from strangers who ask, "Hey Dorothy, where's Toto?" I once lent the cruiser to a female friend, and as we rounded the block on a ride back to my house, a man on the side of the road belted out, "There she is, Miss America!" I've had drug dealers and bums alike compliment me on it. The cruiser is a conversation piece.

During all the cycling I've done on any one of my five bicycles over the past twenty-seven years, one constant has remained: If a dog spots me while I'm pedaling, it will immediately give chase. This is a fact known by all seasoned cyclists.

Panhandlers in Berkeley, California, where I lived on and off for over a year, will do the very same thing if you accidently make eye contact. Guaranteed. So if you intend to avoid confrontation, you must ardently avoid gazing into the eyes of the homeless. Walk in a straight line down the sidewalk on Shattuck Avenue with your focus fixed astutely on the concrete sidewalk directly below your feet. Blast Pandora's "Summer Hits of the 90s" through your oversized headphones—that gargantuan pair of noise-canceling Beats By Dre you purchased specifically for this task, to indicate to the world of beggars that you have muted them out of your life. You're a struggling writer with mounting debt; they probably have more money than you do anyway.

But when riding a bike, it's less easy to avert your eyes from the objects and obstacles you wish to avoid. Visual acuity is a necessary skill of survival while pedaling. Eye contact with a dazed driver pulling out of a parking lot or the delivery truck operator about to pass and then make a right hand turn in front of you can save your life. New cyclists are told to constantly scan their surroundings and to be on the lookout for potential disaster at every moment.

I'm a defensive driver, so I'm naturally a defensive cyclist as well, especially on one of my favorite road rides in the Northeast Kingdom of Vermont. The Lake Willoughby ride is a lollipop route, meaning you travel out and back on the same section of roadway, thus creating the lolli's stick, and then you make a loop in the middle to complete the pop. The pavement on Route 5A, which snakes its way around scenic Lake Willoughby on the loop portion of the pop, provides enough sensory stimulation on its own to keep my brain firing in overdrive. Deep gullies, grass-filled cracks, potholes, low shoulders, gravel, manure piles strewn across the road: Take your pick. And just when I've adjusted to the rhythmic bumping and uneven surfaces, I reach the telltale curve in the road when alarm conditionally sets in as if Pavlov himself is ringing the bell in my ear. Rapidly approaching on the right side of the road is every cyclist's nightmare. It's not a row of tacks or an automated tire shredder or a drunk driver drifting repeatedly onto the shoulder of the road. It's the Dog House.

In my imagination, the Dog House is owned by a nefarious, tattoo-riddled motorcycle gang member who has an entire dresser drawer dedicated to chains and then a whole other drawer dedicated to chain accessories. He spends his leisure hours sharpening knives and shooting squirrels. From the varied and distinct barks that emerge from his property every time I approach, I have concluded that the Dog House proprietor is raising no fewer than twelve angry, flesh-ripping canines purely for sport. Luckily for me, they are all on leashes or behind fences. But each time I ride by, I still employ a Fabian Cancellara-esque time trialing effort to ensure my personal safety. I also clench my water bottle tightly and prepare to spray at will if necessary.

The Nintendo videogame Paperboy, circa 1985, ingrained in me at an early age that every dog, no matter how mellow and well trained, is bound to chase after a moving bicycle, especially if you are trying to deliver newspapers while simultaneously outrunning a tornado and avoiding aggressive break-dancers. It also taught me that garbage cans, storm drains, and even fire hydrants might appear where they are least expected. What I have never been able to figure out, however, is why so many car tires regularly rolled down driveways in that game. Regardless, when I ride my bike, I evoke the spirit of the Paperboy. It is my duty to out pedal the dogs while dodging any and all other hazards, whatever they may be.

I have, even to this day, always successfully eluded the frothy-mouthed, rabid Dog House protectors, but they remind me to stay focused throughout the full duration of the ride. After circumnavigating Lake Willoughby via the Crystal Lake addition one nondescript fall weekday, I was well on my way to the point of the journey where I begin to tell myself I'm practically home. While this juncture in the ride is still a solid seven miles and nearly one thousand feet of climbing away from home, it is the moment that the "You're almost there" mantra begins to play on repeat in my head.

At roughly one mile from that home free marker and the center of the tiny village of West Burke, I caught a glimpse of an unleashed black dog on the left hand shoulder of Route 5. It appeared to be eating fruit that had fallen from a tree, probably apples, so I figured the canine was at least distracted. Still, I kicked my usual Dog House plan into high gear without even realizing, as I unconsciously picked up the pace. I reached down to feel which of my two water bottles was the fullest in case I required arsenal. As I neared the canine that had its back turned to me, I thought to myself, "That is one *big* dog." And right as I passed the big, black dog, it turned its head to meet my eyes. That's when I lost my breath and heartbeat for a moment, because it wasn't a dog at all. It was—instead— a very big, very black bear.

I had lived in Lake Tahoe for two years and saw plenty of bears from the safety of my car's interior. I even moved into an apartment the very next day after a bear had wreaked havoc in the kitchen while the landlord aired out the carpets that were recently cleaned. The landlord warned me of the encounter with the bear and then cautioned, "They'll usually return if they think there's more food." The morning after I moved in, I walked out of the bathroom in a towel to see a bear breathing up against the sliding glass door in my living room. I screamed, locked myself in the bathroom, waited five minutes, and then slowly opened the door inch by inch to reveal that the bear had given up and had moved on to another house. That was the last time I confronted the imminent danger of a sharp-toothed fur monster, and even then I was protected behind two locked doors.

Back on the road, I geared down and started hammering in as aerodynamic a position as possible. When I thought I was well away from the bear, I pulled back my chest, sat up a bit, and cocked my head over my left shoulder. While not exactly close enough to growl down my neck or drool on my rear tire, the bear was still awkwardly galloping down the road just three bike lengths behind me.

A coworker later informed me during a dramatic retelling of the near death experience (yes, almost as dramatic as this one), that black bears do not chase and that I probably just spooked it. Whatever bears "do" and "don't do", this one was close enough and running fast enough to launch me into full-on frenzy mode. I glanced at my speedometer. I was pedaling twenty-four miles per hour. I thought to myself, "I'm on my bike—I can pedal away." It was a similar feeling to the one I had playing summer soccer in Oakland, where reports of gang violence and drive-by shootings were routine. If I rode my bike as fast as I could to the field where we played our games, I figured I could steer clear of the stray bullets in the event that I wound up in any crossfire.

Just when I had convinced myself I was going to be fine while outrunning an agitated bear on my bike, I recalled reading somewhere that bears can run upwards of thirty miles per hour. Realizing that speed was faster than the winner's average over twenty-one days of racing in the Tour de France peloton, I admitted to myself, "I can't pedal that fast," gasped for air, and then prayed for the best.

After propelling my bike as rapidly as I am convinced is possible, I glanced back again to see the image of what was most likely the bear skirting off into the woods, foliage swaying despite no breeze and not a single animal in sight. But the bear's image and the associated fear remained ever present in mind for the rest of the ride. As I cruised into the sleepy hamlet of West Burke, I reminded myself of the universally applicable rule: Never make eye contact with the homeless, whether they are in an urban center or rural regions, rummaging for free fruit off a tree or your restaurant leftovers.

15
Stowe Derby Death March

I longed to race the Stowe Derby, North America's oldest downhill cross-country ski race that begins at the top of the Toll House chairlift at Stowe Mountain Resort and finishes twelve-and-a-half miles later at the community church in town, ever since the February morning my Skidmore College classmate Billy walked into our history colloquium with his arm in a sling and an outrageous story about his epic crash in the annual event. With a start elevation at 3,292 feet and the finish resting just 690 feet above sea level, the race is an alpine skier turned Nordic's dream come true, but one can often lose sight of the forest for the trees.

Billy, an accomplished skier of both disciplines and regular competitor in the event, got confused in the heat of racing and had made a critical error. "On the very first turn of the Stowe Derby," he recalled, "I guess I forgot I was on Nordic skis. I tried to roll my edges over and carve a turn like I would on my alpine gear, and—bam!— broken collarbone." He never even made it to the second turn in the course.

Other events would grab my attention in passing years like the famed Pole Pedal Paddle in Jackson Hole, Wyoming, a multi-leg race including alpine and Nordic skiing along with biking and river travel. But the lure of the Stowe Derby was the strongest, partly because I had a tenuous relationship with the town that I hoped desperately to reconcile but mostly because I thrived on ridiculous competition and had always been tempted by danger.

My first experience with the storybook Vermont ski town of Stowe had taken place roughly twenty-four years earlier on a family trip to the mountain village. The entire Feehan clan, including my extended family of five aunts and uncles and their ten children, embarked on a long weekend of skiing and revelry. While our parents were off ripping around the resort and enjoying hot toddies in the après bar, my cousins and I were forcibly enlisted in the SkiWee army of miniature mountain bombers for the day. I cried and complained and didn't want to be in the lesson because I had to wear a bright yellow bib over my ski jacket so the instructors could identify me as part of the group. I didn't feel cool. And as someone who ultimately carved out a career in the ski industry, I can assure you that success in the sport is based on a mere ten percent skill with the other ninety percent attributed solely to how cool you look. It's certainly worth crying over.

I must have run the tears so much over simply being in the lesson that my dad had completely tuned out my whining when he abandoned me in the program again on the second day so he could go ski on his own. By that point, I wasn't complaining about having to wear the yellow bib anymore. I didn't feel well. I told my dad I was sick first thing in the morning, and he answered with his standard canned response from my childhood that was pulled out the instant any of his three children mentioned a word about not feeling well.

"It's all in your head," he said before walking out the door of the SkiWee room and heading up the chairlift, leaving me in kiddie ski jail for another day.

It wasn't exactly all in my head. I had a raging fever. By mid-morning, the instructors had tracked down my dad on the mountain to come liberate me up from the lesson before I infected any other kids. My throat was so swollen that I was spitting saliva into a towel instead of swallowing by the time my dad came to pick me up. My family packed up the car in the middle of the vacation to return home to New Jersey, where a doctor later confirmed I had an advanced case of Strep throat. My brothers, who were in absolute ski heaven in Stowe, never forgave me for forcing the family to come home early after getting sick. I had obviously planned the whole coup, right down to the day when I was forced to ski with a fever while my throat was ablaze. Siblings can be so ruthless.

"Remember when Christine ruined our ski trip to Stowe?" my brothers would ask as the lead in to retelling this story for the next two decades. They never let me forget how horrible of a little sister I was for getting sick and spoiling all their fun, and any future mention of Stowe always rekindled this recollection as distinctly as that tasty little madeleine cake did for Proust.

To ease the pain of this damning childhood memory, I reasoned that an exhilarating experience at the Stowe Derby could turn the whole thing around and rectify my relationship with the town despite the fact that more than twenty years had gone by. I was a fearless downhill skier who had some experience cross-country skiing, so I thought I was cut out for the event. But before jumping the gun to register for the race, I talked to some other alpine skiing friends who had completed it in the past.

"Oh, the Stowe Derby is the greatest ever!" Greg told me. "You start on top of the mountain, and it's your first time doing it so you'll have a really crappy start number in the back of the field, and you'll go down the trail, and there will be huge ruts at all the turns and you just have to do your damned best to stay upright while you haul past people who are crashing left and right. At the bottom of the trail, there are some ups and downs, and your legs will be so full of lactic acid by then that you'll just want to die, but eventually you hit the Rec Path, and from there it's smooth sailing. I mean, you'll be cruising on the Rec Path to the finish, and that makes all the agony worthwhile. It's the best thing ever!" he reassured me despite the mixed review.

I had owned cross-country ski equipment for three years, although one year it sat idle like most overzealous athletic purchases, the kind where you envision yourself utilizing the gear every waking moment of your life until you actually own the stuff, at which time it takes up permanent residence in your dust-ridden closet. My father was the king of making these kinds of impulse buys: A fly fishing set that was never used in actual water but was regularly deployed on our front lawn while he futilely practiced casting to the mortal embarrassment of his children; a beautiful sculling boat that he abandoned after realizing balance was required to keep it afloat while rowing; and a Peugeot racing bicycle that never made it farther than the Mt. Freedom Golf driving range three miles from home.

My skate ski gear wasn't exactly like that. But I bought it, spent a few days following my graceful, also self-taught roommate Sarah around on some trails, and that was the full extent of my education on skiing technique. I toyed around on it for that first winter, never got out on it the second winter, and then became addicted to its use in the third year of ownership, logging roughly twenty days of huffing and puffing my way around Vermont's finer trail networks.

On the morning of the race, the snow was incredibly soft, as Stowe had received over a foot of the white, fluffy stuff in the twenty-four hours preceding the Derby. My greatest fear before the race was that I was going to fall down while getting off the Toll House chairlift. This was an irrational concern on my part because I get on and off chairlifts nearly every day on alpine ski gear, usually carrying heavy, awkward equipment while also balancing a cup of coffee, but these Nordic toothpicks attached to my feet were so unpredictable. When I got off the chair without an inkling of trouble, I knew I had this whole cross-country thing nailed.

Then the race began, and heat after heat was called to the line.

I poled like a madwoman off the start, crouched low and pulled my arms tight into a tuck, and easily had the lead in my small heat heading into the first switchback. But dear God, I had picked up so much speed and had absolutely no control over my skis as they drifted back and forth between a four-foot wide bobsled track of glazed ice and the haphazard banks of powder that had accumulated on each side of the frozen flume. It took me five seconds of aggressive poling and skating to take a sizeable lead in my pack and only a fraction of that time to explode in a heap of flying equipment and clothing while the other racers all skied passed.

My goggles were full of snow and dangling around my neck while I dug furiously through the powder to find my frosted hat. Had I been a quicker learn, I would have realized much sooner that the Stowe Derby is often one of the clearest living examples of the moral from Aesop's fable *The Tortoise and the Hare*. Slow and steady was the approved method for success. Instead, I continued to enter each sharp turn carrying way too much speed, leading to inevitable destruction and even more lost equipment.

After crashing ten times—yes, ten, and yes, I was counting—I needed to dig deep within my soul for inspiration to get through this miserable experience. Other people were crashing too, but I felt like I was continuously hitting the deck a disproportionate number of times. I was pretty sure I was practically in last place.

That's when I remembered what Greg had said about the Recreation Path portion of the course. If only I could make it to the Rec Path, it would be like coasting on a superhighway to the finish. I floundered up the last grueling hills and slid out of control down their backsides until the terrain began to level off. But the start of the Rec Path Greg had so gloriously boasted about wasn't the superhighway he described. It was a windblown, ungroomed trail of snow that mostly resembled chunky mashed potatoes, and like those who had come before me, I began to trudge along rather slowly without the assistance of gravity. There was no glide. There was only mush, mush, mush.

I found a group of four other folks who were equally disheartened by the condition of the Rec Path, and we began to trade off leads at the front of our pack with the precision of a cycling pace line. After crossing a bridge and being a little unsure of the correct course direction, we identified some markings that lead out into a cold and blustery field of utter misery. Sweating while freezing and exhausted to tears, I thought of the Bataan Death March, and while it was an insulting historical analogy to equate my experience at the Stowe Derby to that of 75,000 American and Filipino prisoners of war, I had hit an all-time low. We eventually made it out of the field and back into the protection of the trees, continuing along the trail until we came to a very familiar bridge.

There was a photographer who I recognized standing in front of it, and I blurted out, "Are we going in circles?"

"Yeah, you were supposed to go left after the bridge instead of right," he replied, and my heart sank even deeper.

When you're on the verge of quitting a physical trial, the last thing you want to realize is that you just added an unnecessary loop onto your journey and have simply ended up back on course where you had previously been ten minutes earlier. Negative progress. By the time I passed a course official who merrily informed me there was, "Only one mile to go!" my verbal filter had completely disengaged.

I exhaled, "Oh, fuck me."

As I puttered across the finish line, emotionally and physically defeated in 314th place with a time of 1:47:08 (the winner having completed the same task nearly a whole hour faster), I despised everything about Nordic skiing. Even some guy who raced the entire course in a full Gumby costume, head to toe, royally destroyed me. I hate losing in general, but I especially hate losing to fictional Claymation characters.

My friend, Bella, who grew up in Stowe and who had also obliterated my time by roughly a half hour, did her very best to offer congratulations in the finish area. She hugged me and said apologetically, "That was absolutely brutal. If it was my first Derby, I'm not sure I would have finished."

I looked at her, shook my head, and replied, "That sucked so much. I absolutely hated every single minute of it." It had been my absolute worst experience on skis ever.

Then I added with the determination of an athlete who simply will not accept defeat, "I can't wait to do it again next year!"

16
Anything To See Lance Armstrong

Before Lance Armstrong became nothing more than a fraud, he was my hero. He had catapulted himself into my life as a sort of idol, and I diligently watched every stage of the Tour de France beginning with his return to the sport in 1999. I purchased a red, white, and blue Trek road bike that was modeled after the same frame he raced on, and I rode it with pride. I read and then recommended that friends read all of his books and pretty much every book ever written about him. I assigned *It's Not About the Bike* to my senior English class as summer reading. And because watching Lance on television just wasn't enough, I hung Annie Liebowitz's naked photograph of Armstrong, taken as a cover shot for an issue of *Vanity Fair*, on my bedroom wall. It was belittling for the male suitors in my life, but I wanted to aim high.

In 2009, my former roommate, Sarah, was planning to spend her summer gallivanting around the old world at the same exact time a ski camp I was coaching on a French glacier was scheduled to finish. We had talked about meeting up in mid-July for a week or so of traveling before I flew home. I had a longstanding dream of seeing a stage of the Tour de France in person, and Lance had just announced his comeback from retirement and intent to compete in that year's edition of the race. It was destiny.

I wanted to travel around Europe with Sarah because she was a hyper planner, the type of person who made a to-do list before brushing her teeth every morning. She was methodical and calculated and rarely did anything without thorough advance consideration. I figured if I traveled with Sarah, the precise route of our trip would be laid out perfectly beforehand, and I could just tag along mindlessly for the ride. It would be like having my very own free tour guide and travel partner in one.

But in May of that year, a solid two months before we planned to meet up at a hostel in Geneva, we were having a difficult time reserving a hotel room in the mountain resort of Verbier for the night before the Tour de France was scheduled to pass through town. Email responses in broken English from Swiss addresses carried harsh news. We were crazy for thinking we would be able to find even a single hotel room or bed in a hostel for anytime during the whole week leading up to the race. Every space in the entire town had been booked up since the official Tour route was announced back in October. Stupid Americans.

When we had nearly given up hope and were beyond sick of being berated by hotel owners over the internet, Sarah received a miraculous email. One establishment, the Hotel Les Touristes, had a room with two beds available for July 18, the night before the stage arrived in town. I logged into their reservation system and tried to book it immediately. Maria, the manager, wrote back to tell me there had been a misunderstanding and the room was not available. I was beginning to realize that travel agents were still useful even in the era of the World Wide Web. After Maria and I exchanged several emails in basic English, she revealed that there was in fact a room available and it would cost each of us fifty bucks to split it with breakfast included. While this was the most expensive room we booked on our whole trip of frugality, it was both the last available room in all of Verbier and likely also the cheapest.

Though I had secured the reservation, I was still apprehensive about the room's availability. I spent the first few days of our trip wondering what we would do if we got all the way to Verbier and had nowhere to sleep. We figured we would just stay up all night or try to befriend some nice European gentlemen with space for us. My mother had shared with me, quite unsolicited, the story of the summer she spent backpacking around Europe when she was in her twenties and found herself a nice German boy. "They're all over the place," she told me. "Two cute American girls—you'll find somewhere to sleep." But we were trying to avoid that kind of eleventh hour decision-making.

It was a rainy morning in Lausanne, Switzerland when we departed for Verbier via a quick stop in Montreux to catch a hint of the world-renowned jazz festival. At the Montreux train station, we put our luggage in a locker and Sarah wasted Swiss franc upon Swiss franc trying to figure out how to lock it. She put the coins in the slot, turned the dial, tried to remove the key, and nothing happened. It was a tiresome travel day, and she was throwing away her coins in order to free us of my wheeled duffel and her backpack. I had never seen Sarah get so mad until the Montreux train station lockers started stealing her money. "It's like ten dollars I just wasted," she huffed. I finally intervened, popped my change in the locker, turned the dial, and pulled out the key with no problem. I couldn't tell if she was pissed at me or relieved.

We walked around a drizzly Montreux, listening to street jazz while eating lunch. After watching a full band perform on our train platform before jumping on the locomotive and making a couple connections, we eventually boarded the St. Bernard Express which took us deep into the valley below Verbier.

From the valley floor, we had to shove our luggage and our bodies in a four-person gondola car to access the village of Verbier. We had the address of our hotel but little sense of how far it was from the center of town. So we began to descend the main street in the village by wandering down the steep switchbacks; I pulled my rolling duffel along and Sarah schlepped her gigantic backpack. Every step we took downhill was calculated as a step back uphill we would eventually have to take with our gear after the completion of the tour stage. Around the turn of an unsuspecting switchback, about two kilometers in distance and several hundred meters in elevation below the gondola station, we found our lodging.

The Hotel Les Touristes was located on the exact road my favorite professional cyclists, including Lance Armstrong, were going to race up the very next day. The tour route meandered immediately outside our hotel's front door. Sarah and I were dumbstruck by our great fortune, and we spent the rest of the evening trying to convince ourselves this was real life and not just a dream. How could we have possibly been so close to not having anywhere to stay only to arrange a totally reasonable hotel room directly on the tour route just weeks before the race?

Over one hundred thousand spectators invaded the town the following morning, crowding the streets and eateries throughout the village. As Sarah and I emerged from beneath our down duvets in our snuggly beds, we realized the splendid luck that had befallen us. Right outside our bedroom window, the massive, inflatable one-kilometer to go banner spanned the roadway. We had hit the Tour de France spectator jackpot.

Prime real estate from which to view the action was going faster than a gentrified SoHo loft, so we scoped out a high-walled switchback that gave us a vantage point of the turn below as well as the one-kilometer mark. Our pleasant innkeeper who gave us free jars of jam but who spoke no English indicated to us in sign language and French (a tongue Sarah claimed to know before the trip but then acted as if she could hardly understand once we got there) that we could store our luggage at the hotel all day long and could use the facilities whenever needed during the course of the race. We abandoned our bags at the hotel and set up camp at ten in the morning alongside a European couple who had plenty of wine, bread, and cheese to share with us throughout the day.

Sarah and I enjoyed the fanfare of the pre-Tour circus spectacle, but we were both anxiously awaiting the arrival of Lance. After more than four hours of sitting in the hot sun, drinking wine, and making friendly conversation with an American expatriate who had written for the cycling magazine *VeloNews*, we were ready to see some bike racing. The television helicopter hovered nearby, and we could make out what appeared to be a rider wearing an Astana team kit weaving around the switchback below us. Astana was the team Lance rode for, but it was also the team of another race favorite—Alberto Contador, the sneaky Spaniard—and either one of them could have had the lead as they approached the summit finish in Verbier.

"How will we know if it's Lance?" Sarah asked.

I replied, "He's the only guy on the team wearing a black and yellow helmet. Everybody else wears team-issued Astana helmets, but Lance has the Livestrong colors on his." That's when Alberto Contador came riding around the turn dancing on his pedals with a look of grit smeared across his face. Without hesitation, Sarah hit the start button on her stopwatch so we would know Lance's exact split to catch Contador. As seconds ticked by and the lead became minutes, we yielded our hope for the American dream to come true. It was the day our music died. Armstrong eventually rounded the bend with the support of another one of his teammates, Andreas Klöden, but all hope for the overall victory had been lost that afternoon on the climb to Verbier.

The results felt devastating, but not as devastating as the trudge we still had back to the gondola station while carrying our luggage through that crowd of one hundred thousand people. We earnestly weighed the option of walking down the mountain to Le Châble train station and reasoned it was roughly seven kilometers of gravity-assisted walking versus the two kilometer twisting, turning uphill climb. The shorter distance won out, and we began the hike. I lost Sarah amidst the chaos for several minutes when she unexpectedly stopped to take a picture of a traditional Swiss horn band.

It was scorching hot, profuse sweating made the shirt stick to my back, and fellow members of the swarm kept walking into the duffel that lagged just behind my ankles. Sarah was stealthy and agile and able to make the necessary jukes and dodges to advance our position through the sea of people. As we approached the queue for the gondola, I had flashbacks to my childhood when I demanded a ride on Disney World's Space Mountain despite the never-ending line that snaked along for what seemed like miles. But we were in Europe now, and I had just come off nearly three weeks of studying the local custom of elbowing people and planting my poles in front of skiers in lift lines at Les Deux Alpes.

Sarah was equally skilled at the subtle art of European line negotiation. So we began to assert our presence and fill in gaps wherever they appeared. A group of American guys who were roughly our age realized we had overtaken them when we came face-to-face on one of the double-backed rows, Sarah and I now clearly ahead of them. "Hey!" one of them shouted, "You're like totally cutting."

I was amused by his ignorance, chuckled to Sarah, and replied, "We're kind of pros at this." An hour later we boarded a gondola and returned to the valley below. The long train ride back to Geneva still loomed on the horizon and our day was barely halfway over at that

LIFE GIVES ME LEMONS

point. Sarah and I split up at the train station to go our separate ways as she carried on to Gimmelwald, and I backtracked to the big city on a short solo adventure before flying home.

For years after the trip, I emoted a genuine sense of loyalty and accomplishment because I could tell people that I dragged an insanely heavy bag on the trains all over Switzerland just to see Lance Armstrong race the fifteenth stage of the Tour de France, his comeback event where he ultimately finished on the podium in third place. I was a true fan.

But after his name was disgraced when he finally admitted that the doping allegations that had haunted him throughout his entire career were valid, I couldn't help but feel gutted for ever idolizing him. It was a slap in the face to conclude that I had wasted so many hours following his tour of lies and deceit, and his dark confession sullied my every memory of that serendipitous trip to Verbier. I pulled the bare-skinned photograph of Lance off my bedroom wall and painfully admitted to myself that my hero was nothing more than a clever, manipulative, egomaniacal fraud, who happened to ride a bicycle.

17
The Spontaneously Exploding Rental Car

No matter what I do to pay the bills, my job always sounds exorbitantly more glamorous in theory than it ever is in reality. I don't mean to whine more than I already do, but when I'm sprinting through a major international airport à la *Home Alone* dragging both oversized and overweight duffel and ski bags behind me with heavy plastic boots swinging back and forth across my shoulders, I'm rarely as excited about the trip as I would be to venture on a traditional ski vacation.

Aside from one weekend in Mt. Tremblant, the last genuine ski vacation I was on, with no work and no racing involved, was a family trip to Vail in 1997. On that trip, I had to skip two breathtaking days of skiing under bluebird Colorado skies to finish writing a paper on William McKinley for the sophomore history class I was missing in order to take the vacation. An anarchist assassinated McKinley during his second presidential term, and I kept thinking if only it had happened sooner in his life my paper could have been done in just one day. It took McKinley nine days to eventually die of gangrene after being shot twice in the gut, and I sacrificed those optimal days of skiing at my most beloved resort in the world in order to demonstrate to my teacher that I was capable of both researching facts on America Online and then citing them in a coherent paper. If only I had known back then how precious and elusive a ski vacation would prove to be in my future, I would have pumped out that McKinley rag during the flight.

Everyone mistakes almost every day of my work for vacation. As much as I gloat over the jealousy of other people, the misunderstanding still irks me to no end. Just because I regularly pack a suitcase and then toil at some of the world's most renowned ski resorts, that doesn't mean I'm on perpetual holiday. If it would help alter the perspective of strangers, I can start traveling with a brief-case, though I'm not sure I have anything to put in it. I work too, and sometimes my workdays challenge my patience much the same as yours.

This particular spring morning started earlier than most before five, cozy in bed in Norwich, Vermont, where I had recently relocated but had not yet unpacked my life before I had to travel to Copper Mountain, Colorado for a ten-day recruiting trip at a national championship event. I awoke in the pitch dark, showered quietly with a still sleeping roommate on the other side of the bathroom wall, threw together a carry-on, tossed some bags in the back of my Subaru, dialed in the GPS, turned on the radar detector, and cruised down the interstate toward Boston for my flight. A meager travel budget had once again prevented me from securing a hotel room near the airport the night before flying, but it certainly wasn't the end of the world. I could roll.

After an extra special suspected terrorist pat down, no major delays, one pesky layover in Chicago, and a second flight, I landed in Denver by early afternoon. I had to transfer all aforementioned luggage onto a shuttle bus, and then I was delivered to the counter of a nationally recognized rental car agency. My reservation was for a smaller sized sport utility vehicle so I could make the nearly two-hour drive to Copper Mountain where I would hopefully convince a handful of snowboarders to enroll in the school that paid my salary. I was heading into the mountains, and people who live in the mountains leave their snow tires on until May for good reason, so a standard car likely wouldn't suffice.

Of course, the rental company had no remaining small SUVs in the fleet despite my reservation, so I was offered a free upgrade from the fuel-efficient Toyota Rav4 to an unnecessarily cumbersome Chevy Traverse. Despite my affinity for Japanese vehicles, the Chevy was shiny and new with only sixteen thousand miles on it, so I diffused my vehicular bigotry for the time being.

As I pulled onto the highway with my windows down and old school hip-hop blasting on the radio, I felt pretty baller. A guy in a Jeep Cherokee drove alongside me and gave me a "Hey there!" head nod. I had arrived. In retrospect, ski friends would later point out that the name of the vehicle alone—Chevy Traverse—should have raised my advisory system threat level from low green to high orange. Nobody likes traversing. It's slow and requires extreme effort.

My trip coincided precisely with an emergency closure of Interstate 70, the primary route from Denver to Copper, due to rock blasting on the highway. You've seen those "Warning: Falling Rocks" signs? Well, sometimes highway workers plan when the rocks are going to fall, and that requires a road closure. While this may have thwarted the plans of less skilled travelers, I proceeded on an alternate route that should have doubled the distance of my journey. As I proceeded along Interstate 70 through Denver and then headed southwest toward the town of Fairplay, an adorably rugged fellow in a pickup truck offered a gratuitous peace sign; I smiled back. He waved. The almost four-hour drive after a day of air travel meant nothing. I felt like a millions dollars.

I was making decent time on Highway 9, up the switchbacks between Alma and Blue River, as I traveled steadily in a line of cars chugging along at forty miles per hour. My progress had propelled me to within an hour of my destination, and I could smell the finish line as boldly as a bouquet of fresh cut roses. I was desperately looking forward to a long, hot shower and a rejuvenating nap before dinner.

As suddenly as the word suddenly implies, my Chevy Traverse, driving smoothly along in the caravan, jerked and clunked and halted to an abrupt, fortuitous crawl. The sound of grinding metal permeated my ear canal as a plume of thick, white smoke funneled simultaneously from beneath the hood and through the tailpipe. A miracle alone enabled me to quickly redirect the front end of the vehicle to the road's slim shoulder, where I wedged the Traverse between the traffic lane and a towering snow bank.

My first thought was, "The car is on fire!" My second thought was, "And all these assholes behind me are driving right by!" The parable of the Good Samaritan notwithstanding, I had to wait for a string of egocentric drivers to pass before it was even safe to open my driver's side door and escape the damaged car. As I emerged from the vehicle, I realized that it was not on fire but it might as well have been. Every fluid that enables a car to run was puddled behind the vehicle and various engine parts including connecting rods, bolts, and pieces of the block were scattered in the roadway. It looked like a child's Build Your First Engine toy kit if all the pieces had been smashed with a hammer prior to packaging.

A passing department of transportation worker stopped to offer assistance and nearly died of laughter surveying the engine's debris. It was a good thing he actually stopped, because my cell phone had no reception and no other passersby expressed any interest in lending a helping hand. "Oh!" he exclaimed as he jumped from his truck. "Your car is totally fucked." Then he pulled out his cell phone to take pictures of the parts in the road before finally phoning for help.

In full disclosure, this wasn't the first time a vehicle I was driving came to a sudden, unexpected stop in the middle of operation. I had some previous experience with an exploding engine in the past, as that Frankencar my dad bought for me back in high school once did the same exact thing, minus the smoke and parts actually falling onto the road. The seedy used car salesman had disconnected the oil indication light, among others, in the dashboard before selling us the car. Less than six months into driving it, my oil pump went, but I had no idea anything was wrong until I threw an engine rod one morning while driving to school. I prayed the car was totaled so I could get a new one, but a warranty meant the seller had to replace the engine, and I had to continue to drive the car with no heat or radio. Not my luckiest day, and neither was this.

Twenty minutes after the road worker called for help, a coffee carrying deputy from the bustling metropolis of Alma, Colorado arrived to perform his civic duty of directing traffic around the metal heap in the road. They both laughed even louder once I told them it was a rental. I used the road worker's phone to call the agency's roadside assistance number, and that's when I was informed I had to wait an hour for a wrecker that would then drive me another hour out of the way to their office at the Eagle County Airport.

"No way," I said. "I'm leaving the car here, and I'll pick up another one tomorrow." I had been traveling for fifteen hours straight at that point and was hitting the limit of my patience. I could feel the lid on my can of swears about to burst wide open. Instead of getting snippy, I hung up on the rental car representative and moved on to solving my transportation crisis.

My coworker, Jamie, who had arrived in Colorado the previous week, thankfully accepted the rescue mission as little more than an inconvenient diversion from his relaxing afternoon in Copper. He picked me up on the side of the road, and we abandoned the smoldering pile of scrap metal with the cop and road worker, still giggling like two schoolboys while they awaited the arrival of a tow-truck.

The next day, when I hitched a ride with one of the snowboarder's parents to the nearest facility to replace my rental car, the only four-wheel drive vehicle available in stock was another free upgrade to a Chevy Suburban, a vehicle even larger than the Traverse. Whatever became of that oh so reliable SUV I had originally received? Turns out it had a recall that the rental company had overlooked, hence the spontaneously combusting engine. The discount applied for my aggravation went directly into the pocket of my employer, and I was still over budget on fuel for the trip. So much for those free upgrades.

18

Internet Dating for Shallow Idiots

Every time I was around my friend Lola, I would end up reactivating an online dating profile without remembering how much I despised online dating. I'm simply not cut out for it, but she never seemed to remember. It's the only influence Lola has had over me that I find disconcerting. The drinking, the staying up way too late debating inconsequential topics like whether *16 and Pregnant* is a better show than *Dance Moms*, and the excessive baking of high-fat treats while we shared a house for a few months together were all forgivable offenses. But the very concept of internet dating is in fundamental opposition to how I believe people should interact in this world, and Lola would never let it go.

I have heard that plenty of folks find a future mate using online services. I once attended a wedding where the couple getting married and two additional parties in attendance had all met on Match.com. I'm willing to admit that valid success stories have emerged from using the services. There are also probably cases where people meet their future spouses while incarcerated or at drug rehabilitation; it doesn't mean that was something I was willing to try. Though perhaps I should have considered it, especially since my personal online dating history proved less than encouraging in totality.

I have the uncanny ability to attract a wide variety of men via an online profile who would never think twice about approaching me in a public setting but who feel perfectly comfortable soliciting me over the internet. I know I'm supposed to be flattered by all the attention, but on more than one occasion I became the target of a deep-seated hatred against good-looking women who wouldn't give the less attractive men of the world a fighting chance. It got ugly and frightening, and I usually ended up deleting my account within twenty-four hours of creating it. When I utilized politeness and honesty and it was met with invective and cheap shots, I could get pretty fired up. The fifty-year-old who lived a hundred miles away, smoked, and had been divorced multiple times wasn't exactly a potential lover in my eyes. But the bachelor world had a hard time understanding that the reason I was available into my early thirties wasn't simply because no one had asked to be my boyfriend.

I wasn't a diamond in the rough who had slipped through the cracks. I was single because my expectations were high, and I was still looking for someone who embodied passion, charm, intelligence, and that inexplicable fire within. A former college roommate and I referred to that unique but somewhat indescribable characteristic as chimichanga, because no word could suitably express the almost palpable quality that made me undeniably attracted to certain people. Without the chimichanga, I was flying solo.

Despite Lola's insistence that internet dating is a worthwhile pursuit, she is still amazing. If you ever have the opportunity to live with her, you might be lucky enough to wake up one Saturday morning to a house full of half-naked professional bike racers strewn across every square inch of the floor. When you open the front door of your house, you may even notice one of their cars parked on your front lawn. You can walk into your home on a random Wednesday evening to find a drunken dance party and impromptu fashion show taking place in your living room. Or you'll discover a blue Post-It Note stuck to the cover of *The Joy of Sex: A Gourmet Guide to Love Making (Complete and Unabridged Illustrated Edition)* with a suggestion like this: "CJ – How about you write an update to this book? I'd buy it! –L."

I went to Boulder to visit Lola who had recently moved there for graduate school, and within hours I found myself hunting down eligible gentlemen in the greater Denver area. No surprise there, I was bored. Nothing was panning out on the Colorado front because I was just browsing without a clear focus. In short, I was surveying the scene in my online shopping for dudes.

Then something curious happened. I began to receive a plethora of messages from pretty cool guys back East. Despite the fact that in my profile I acknowledged I was "honest to a fault" and confessed that the most private thing I was willing to share was that "I look at the pictures first, and sometimes I forget to recycle," cute New England men still desired my attention. Sure, there were the creepers too, but they were easy enough to ignore. Or so I thought.

A certain level of skepticism is required for safe and effective online dating. I had heard too many horror stories about people falling deeply in love with frauds, sometimes at the expense of being scammed out of money, and I was familiar with the term catfishing that describes this modern day phenomenon. I had friends recount tales of meeting people in person who they couldn't even recognize as the girl or guy from the dating profile. Photoshop is dangerous for so many reasons, not excluding romances of the heart.

One message I received on my account while still in Colorado was particularly interesting. It was a multi-paragraph introduction from a user who had no personal data filled out and no pictures available in his profile. But his introductory email certainly seemed convincing. He wrote, "Hello super spiffy green mountain skier and biker! You seem quite approachable and personable, and I absolutely love the impression of you I get from a good look at your pics so here I am! I've just made my profile, but with that, I think if you just don't appeal to someone, why waste the whole profile/photo thing? Meanwhile if they ARE in fact intrigued, they will probe deeper, including asking to see pictures, which I have and would readily message on over! The name's Ken. Thirty-two years of age. Reside in Keene, though am originally from an hour north of the Bronx (to have been a Sox fan woulda been equal to sacrilege!). A Gemini. Left-handed. Outgoing and fun loving. Quick witted and random. Loyal and reliable. Affectionate and cuddly. Usually nice company as I have a wide array of interests and am always game for new experiences! Should on this beautiful weekend you find you might like to communicate with me and learn more, I would in turn find that a reply from you made my entire day."

Call me a sucker, but I took the bait. This was before I had learned that many people on dating sites send form messages out in mass looking for any bite. The social predators create a Mad Libs form and fill in just enough detail to make you think you're someone special in their eyes. Hook, line, and sinker, I replied, "Definitely need to see pictures. I believe personalities must match as well, but I'm a very visual person. Thanks for the note."

Ken responded so quickly that it was as if he had been sitting in front of his computer awaiting my response with bated breath. He offered up his email address so I could search for his Facebook page before adding, "If still interested, write me back. If not, hey I realize I'm not gonna be everyones cup of tea."

The grammar mistakes were starting to unnerve me, but I decided to look up his Facebook profile anyway since he presented himself as an open and honest individual. I believe quality writing is a sign of both aptitude and attention to detail, but I can be forgiving in that department as both a former teacher and the loving daughter and sister of men who struggle with spelling and writing. I'm a wordsmith, but I'm not a grammar stickler, especially if positive qualities and attractiveness can fill in the gaps. After typing his email address into the Facebook search box, I instantly found his picture.

I'm afraid that what I was viewing was, indeed, his Super 8 Motel uniform and not a Halloween costume. He was considerably overweight, had a full beard and wore glasses, and the only picture he had of himself was taken with the camera attached to the computer at his place of employment. His activities and interests included, "Spending time with my son, card games, board games, trivia games, mini golf, snow tubing, Christmas Tree Shops, and going to the ocean." The only thing we shared in common was an appreciation for the music of the Red Hot Chili Peppers and the radio program *This American Life*. Definitely not my type.

I've often sought the proper way to let men down gently while also clearly indicating that I'm not interested—not one bit—not in a million years—not if we were the last two people on Earth—not even saying there's a chance. I don't want to leave someone expectantly awaiting my reply for days when I have no interest in responding, so I decided to play along with Ken's cup of tea colloquialism. I chose my words cautiously and wrote back, "Thanks again for your note, but yeah, I'm not really up for tea. Best of luck in your search."

I thought this was a transparent and yet still positive manner in which to send him on his way to find the true love of his life. I'm sure she's out there somewhere, much closer to Keene, much more attracted to Ken, and way more into snow tubing than I am. But Ken had an afterthought for me. After receiving my message, he countered, "I dont dig idiots that try to cover up their shallowness with lame wit. Bye."

Ouch.

I don't dig people who insult me while forgetting to use apostrophes in contractions, but I was trying not to hold that against him until this reply. I always thought of myself as someone who had much to offer and a lot of love to give, but even I knew my dating limits. Let's get real here, if only for a moment. I spend the vast majority of my time skiing down icy mountains and pedaling bikes around the world. What did he think we were going to do, play Dungeons & Dragons before browsing store aisles to complete our joint collection of miniature golf-themed Christmas ornaments? He tried to cut me deep, and it was wholly uncalled for. I would rather not throw the last dagger, but in this instance I couldn't resist.

I collected my thoughts and penned this final response that has since become nothing shy of legendary among friends. Straight at Ken, a complete stranger, I hurled these words with reckless abandon: "You live over fifty miles away from me, never went to college, have a kid, and I'm not the least bit attracted to you. I was trying to be kind; but since you decided to play the asshole card, I rescind my best wishes. Try playing in your own league next time."

I never heard from Ken again. He had finally been silenced, and I was free to delete my profile and move on to real life interactions. Unsurprisingly, karma kept me on the dating bench for quite some time over that one, but it was all worth it in hindsight. Some people just aren't cut out for online dating, and it turns out I was one of them. After enduring some limited episodes of heartache, the chairlift at a Colorado ski resort proved to be my preferred scene.

19
A Not-So-Optional Kayak Rack

My father's family has owned a house in the resort community of Highland Lakes, New Jersey since the fifties, and the modest log cabin on the main lake still serves as a summer meeting destination for all of my relatives. As kids, my brothers and I spent weeks at a time at the lake house with our grandmother who taught us to play five hundred rummy on rainy days and let us row and paddle boats all over the lake when the sun was shining. Despite the drafts through the walls and creaking floorboards under foot, the lake house remains one of my favorite houses in the entire world.

I was living through a lonely spring in Killington, Vermont when I decided that riding my bike every afternoon wasn't providing the necessary variety of fitness I sought in my daily routine. Coworkers had kayaks and paddleboards, and a nearby reservoir with a public boat launch made for easy access to a clean waterway. I decided one sunny afternoon after borrowing a colleague's kayak to paddle around the reservoir that it was high time I became a boat owner. It had been years since

I last rowed that rusty aluminum vessel off my grand-mother's dock, a boat that sat upside-down in her drive-way for years before finally losing its sea worthiness to worn out holes, but I could recall with clarity the con-nection I always felt to the water. Boat ownership was bound to return me to those carefree childhood after-noons at the lake house.

My visions of paddling weren't the least bit grandiose. I never imagined myself careening off water-falls or dodging rocks in whitewater. When I envisioned a fun day of boating, it involved me steadily paddling a kayak on serene flat water, the greatest danger a slim pos-sibility of encountering a cantankerous water snake or ornery lake monster. That had already happened to me once on a vacation in North Carolina when I discovered a snake dangling off my paddle as I pulled it mid-stroke from a swampy inlet, so I knew to constantly scan the placid waters of the Woodward Reservoir for reptiles and eels and whatever other slimy creatures might try to hitch a ride while I pushed along.

But first, I needed a boat. I had become a fan of Craigslist for purchasing big-ticket items, and the posts on the site revealed a handful of folks in Vermont who hastily bought kayaks and then never used them. I swore that wouldn't be me; I would be different. I wouldn't buy a piece of sporting equipment just to let it sit completely idle. And I certainly wouldn't list it for sale on Craigslist a year after I bought it.

Unfortunately, most of the Craigslist sellers demanded a value so close to the original purchase price that it wasn't practical to buy a kayak from any one of them. I could put the boat in the water and discover a hole, and then I'd be out a giant pile of cash. If people recognized the inherent risk in making secondhand purchases with no return policy, they would realize that the majority of prices on Craigslist are simply foolish. A new car depreciates an average of eleven percent when it's driven off the lot, and another fifteen to twenty-five percent each year over the first five years of ownership. That kayak someone paid a grand for and stored in a shed for two years isn't the same boat I would buy in a store right now, so no, I won't offer a penny more than six hundred dollars despite the asking price of eight fifty.

Once I determined it was best to buy the boat in a traditional brick and mortar storefront, I began exploring exactly what kind of kayak I desired. I already had too many cluttered rack configurations between storage boxes and bike trays, and the last thing I wanted to do was buy another toy that required its own roof attachment for transport. My Subaru Outback was spacious enough to fit my coworker's kayak inside and even close the hatchback, so I measured her boat. So long as the kayak was less than ten feet in length, it would fit just fine.

When my brothers were lucky enough to be in the Boy Scouts while I had to sell Thin Mints, we made frequent trips to Ramsey Outdoor Store in a nearby town to stock up on camping supplies for their adventures. On a visit home to see my family, I peeked my head in to the outdoor store because they had an advertised boat sale. The Old Town Otter XT was a little over nine feet long and featured bold streaks of yellow, orange, and red on its exterior. It was a beautiful vessel. It was meant to be my boat.

When the store clerk tried to sell me an accompanying roof rack, I turned him down and confidently stated, "I'm buying this kayak specifically because I can fit it inside my car without a rack."

I fancied myself a bit of a genius.

After all, I had beaten the entire sales system of the outdoor sports industry by refusing to cave to yet another roof accessory. The boat fit smoothly in the back of my car, but I did lose the ability to use all but one passenger seat with the kayak in there. It was the aptly named lonesome spring, though, so my limited car capacity didn't make much difference.

Once summer rolled around, all that started to change. The weather finally broke and friends from afar wanted to visit my Vermont resort town to recreate and relax and enjoy the natural scenery. A fellow outdoorsman and writer, Bryan was somewhat of a kindred spirit who came to spend a long weekend in Killington. I wanted to take him out on the water, so I borrowed my coworker's boat to use along with my own, and that's when I realized a kayak rack probably would have been handy.

We could put one boat in each of our cars and drive to the reservoir, no problem, but I fiercely wanted to solve the puzzle so we could get to the water in only a single vehicle. Bryan threw ropes across one kayak on my roof while I loaded another in the backseat. A passing car pulled into my driveway, and someone jumped out to ask for what I assumed would be directions.

"Can you help me unscramble the names of these Ben & Jerry's flavors?" he asked before realizing the peculiarity of his question. "It's for a scavenger hunt."

While I decoded Chunky Monkey and Vanilla Heath Bar Crunch, a female passenger in the car emerged with a proposition for Bryan.

"What would it take for me to convince you to shave your beard?" she asked.

"I'll shave my beard," he replied, "but I don't have a razor."

The scavenger hunt participants had started that morning in Boston and were already in Vermont by mid-afternoon. This was a most serious contest.

"I have my razor," I mentioned half in passing. Moments later, Bryan emerged from my apartment after having shaved his face using my Gillette Venus Spa Breeze leg razor, complete with pink gel bars. The hunters snapped their after photo and drove off in a hurry.

"The weirdest things happen when we're together," I observed. The weirdest things really did happen to us. The previous day we had received complimentary tickets to ride the alpine slide at a nearby ski resort when I caught the sales attendant reading one of the articles I had written for the weekly town gazette. Bryan and I had also made an appearance on the front page of a local newspaper one winter when we met up to go ice skating together while visiting our respective families in New Jersey over Christmas vacation. By the time we were finished hanging out, we almost always emerged with a new story to tell.

Bryan, now clean-shaven in my driveway, couldn't secure the front end of the kayak to any part of my car, and it seemed destined to catch wind and blow right off my roof once we tried to drive. It just wasn't worth the risk, so after an hour of maneuvering boats and the surprise scavenger hunt, we conceded to driving both cars to go kayaking.

"If only you had a kayak rack…" Bryan noted as we shuttled the boat from my roof and into the back of his Jeep Cherokee.

How proud I had been of my mastermind plan to accommodate transporting all the toys for my outdoor pursuits in a medium-sized Subaru. It was flawless up until the moment I had a friend tag along, but that was the only instance I encountered when I had to move two boats at the same time. Freedom was the ability to pack everything I needed in that single space. I had moved across the country from California to Vermont bearing only one load of possessions that could fit in my car. If it didn't fit in the car, it didn't make it. That summer in Killington turned to fall and fall turned to winter and winter turned to delayed spring, and I decided to move across the state. Suddenly, I had to consolidate all of my toys in the car in as few trips as possible.

I had already relocated one full carload to my new house a little over an hour away and was rounding back for a second trip. This one was reserved for adventure gear, and I had loaded skis and bikes in their appropriate roof racks. The back of the Subaru was empty, and the time had come to toss my kayak inside. Carrying the boat over my shoulder, I somehow miscalculated my own strength upon reaching the vehicle and literally hurled the kayak into the back of the car. It slid over the folded seats with noticeable force and did not slow down until it abruptly met and then crashed clear through windshield, leaving a gaping hole and spider-web shatter mark behind.

Determined to transport the kayak inside my car instead of with the aid of a roof rack, I had accidentally propelled the boat straight through my windshield.

Despite the fact that I had planned to trade the car in and purchase a new one in a few months, I still had to shell out over two hundred dollars to replace the windshield. After talking with a colleague who offered an industry discount on roof racks, I eventually yielded and bought a rather snazzy one of those for my new car at the very reasonable price of eighty bucks. My great kayak deal was becoming less awesome by the day.

That same summer, the paddleboard craze developed in full force, and a number of my pals started paddling while standing upright. I felt diminutive and on a totally different, if not inferior, plane paddling in my kayak next to my towering friends. Once they persuaded me to try a standup paddleboard, I was instantly hooked like a junkie on Meth. The kayak no longer produced the same high, and I found myself listing both the boat and its accompanying roof rack on Craigslist with complete recognition that I was, in fact, one of those people I swore I would never become. The kayak had brought such bad luck that the paddleboard was destined to provide greater happiness.

The very first day I took my brand new board out on the Connecticut River was positively affirming of my decision to swap the kayak. After launching from the Dartmouth College boathouse and paddling north up the river, I had to continually remind myself that I was not Huckleberry Finn. I was entirely lost in the fantasy of synchronized paddle strokes and whipping waves cresting the top of the board as I lived free of rules and responsibility on the prismatic Mississippi in my mind.

After nearly two hours of using my arm muscles that sat dormant all winter, I jumped on to the rickety

Ledyard dock and crouched down to lift the board out of the water. My exhausted Tyrannosaurus arms were no match for the slippery and oddly weighted paddleboard. With my strength left behind in the river, I struggled to pull the thirty-pound load up on the dock. I lost my grip for just a second, and the brand new fiberglass craft clumsily fell atop two protruding screws, leaving perfectly round punctures in the bottom of my precious board and crushing my spirits in an instant.

While all hope for the rig was not lost and a return to flotation was a quick epoxy repair away, the cosmetic damage was permanent, as was my realization that my luck had nothing to do with the kayak in the first place. The shape of the boat made little difference if I was captain at the helm.

20
How to Run Yourself Over With Your Own Car

There are certainly things I have said and done that I regretted for a moment, a few hours, maybe even a whole day. I can be too lazy to recycle, often put my foot in my mouth, and once embarrassed all of my favorite coworkers by publicly desecrating the painting of a dead woman. On at least one occasion, I have consumed just enough alcohol to impair my judgment without imbibing quite enough to wholly prevent me from being rude to people I don't even know. When a vertically challenged gentleman called me out for cutting him in line outside a dance club in Burlington one night, I asked him in all seriousness if he was, by any chance, absolutely amazing in bed to compensate for his Napoleonic stature. I thought it was a backhanded compliment, but he wasn't even remotely amused.

Once in my life, I did something so disturbing that, to this day, I still harbor the very deepest regret that burns at my soul.

Not everyone is talented enough to run themselves over with their own car. It requires a precise combination of intrepid skill and careless stupidity. A cold March night, a few glasses of white wine, a reunion with a close friend who had moved out West for the year, and a dark drive up a frozen, rutted dirt road in rural Vermont (where the only law enforcement official, Phil the Constable, moonlights as the town drunk) might just provide the proper planetary alignment for success in this endeavor. A house party smack in the middle of a week of ski races at which you get to watch your favorite people in the whole world compete in a drinking game that involves picking up a paper bag using only their mouths while their hands are clasped behind their backs can prove simply inspirational. It also helps if your car is both possessed and hates your freaking guts.

From the moment I decided it was time to sell my car and buy a new one, the 2002 Subaru Outback that had faithfully transported both me and the contents of my life over tens of thousands of miles all over the country got mad. Okay, not just mad, but exceptionally pissed. Its anger manifested itself in a number of strange occurrences that started just after I had to replace the windshield when I pitched the kayak through it.

After a family vacation to the Outer Banks, my brother was piloting the Subaru up the Garden State Parkway when we heard a loud pop like a gunshot. Tony Soprano was nowhere to be seen, so I doubted we had taken any mob fire. I thought we had blown a tire, but my brother Kevin had no difficulty controlling the car. He pulled over to the shoulder of the highway, and I got out to examine the vehicle. That's when I noticed the sunroof had mysteriously exploded. All the glass was still intact inside the frame of the sunroof, but it was shattered into a thousand tiny pieces. There was no clear point of contact as if a rock or piece of debris had struck the car. The auto glass expert would later tell me he had never seen anything like it, and that it appeared the glass had exploded from the inside out.

After repairing the sunroof—indeed, my second glass purchase of the season—I somehow managed to completely destroy the fuel and exhaust systems, front to back, totaling over three thousand dollars worth of damage, by driving over an unmarked, snow-covered boulder while backing out of my friend's driveway at night. Clearly, the car knew it was headed for the chopping block.

When my Subaru turned against me for the absolute worst and started to remind me a little too much of the red Pontiac Fury from the Stephen King novel *Christine*, I had the unique opportunity to run myself over with it. I cite this as a unique opportunity not because it was original or creative in any particular way. As it turns out, plenty of people make the same miscalculation that led to my car leveling and then dragging me down a dark, dirt road without a driver. The bit that makes my story distinct among the rest is the simple fact that I am still alive. Many other people who forget to lock the transmission before stepping out of their vehicle, from professional cyclist Xavier Tondo of Spain to Virginia Bustamente of Houston, Texas, have not survived a similar misstep. And those who do survive typically suffer grave, traumatic injuries requiring surgery.

I admit that the story sounded almost too heroic the following morning in Bailey's & Burke, the country store with amazing breakfast sandwiches in the middle of a no-stoplight town, as I regaled my friends with the tale while suffering from a yet undiagnosed concussion and knee injury. I did have some clue about the knee injury. I couldn't bear an ounce of weight on my right leg and was convinced I had suffered the standard skier's injury—a blown out knee, consisting of a torn anterior cruciate ligament—with my antics from the night before. In a long athletic career of soccer, lacrosse, skiing, and Thanksgiving Day tackle football with male cousins, I had somehow managed to dodge the seemingly inevitable ACL tear. An orthopedist once told me I had unusually hardy yet elastic ligaments for a woman.

But there was nothing heroic about getting my all-wheel drive Subaru stuck on ice with its four tires spinning while exhaust poured out the tailpipe into the frosted March nightscape the previous evening. I tried every trick in the book from the usually reliable floor mat traction tactic to aggressive drive and reverse rocking, all to no avail. In an act of desperation, I phoned a friend who was spending the night in a condo just up the road. Damsel in distress is not a role I play with ease, yet I pleaded for a rescue from Jeff. He showed up a few minutes later, quickly assessed the situation, and got behind the car to offer a manly push. The car pulled right off the ice with his effort, but he continued to jog behind the car with his hands on the bumper even after I was freed. I was ecstatic to be out of the tight jam, and I wanted to both thank him for his help and tell him I was all set. The light on my gear console had recently burned out making it difficult to see what I was doing in the dark. In the flurry of the moment, I shifted into neutral, opened the driver's door, and stepped out of the car.

Cars on hills don't stay in one place while in neutral. They roll in the downhill direction, contouring the fall line, much like an out of control downhill ski racer in the midst of a high-speed crash. As my car proceeded to reverse itself down the road, my initial reaction from the driver's doorway was to use my superhuman strength to hold back the one-ton, ghost-driven vehicle headed for off-road doom. There are stories of everyday people exhibiting extreme physical abilities in life and death situations, and a simple Google search on the subject will offer a mighty convincing list of evidence to suggest I was only moderately insane for instinctively thinking I could stop the car using my own body weight.

Conventional wisdom prevailed in this case, and instead of holding the car back by bracing myself against the door, I was, instead, flat-out leveled by it. After falling to the ground and striking my head distressingly on the ice, I found myself tightly wedged between the roadway and the undercarriage of the vehicle with my right leg bent backwards beneath my body. This position would lead to painful meniscus damage, but it would also ultimately prevent my leg from being crushed by my car's front tire. I was caught under the Subaru and dragged across the ground while it rolled backwards down the dirt road until Jeff—the real hero of the tragedy—jumped over my body and through the open door of the moving vehicle, Hollywood stuntman-style, and shifted the car into the safest gear of all: Park.

From underneath the car, it felt like this took whole minutes for the vehicle to finally stop moving. In reality, it was mere seconds. But I had so forcefully struck my head when the car door took me out that I was in a daze.

Even after the car was no longer moving, it still felt like it was. And then I uttered the most brilliant words of the night. Railed with pain and stunned by a head injury, I couldn't imagine how I was going to get out from underneath my devilish Subaru.

"I'm stuck. You're going to have to drive the car off of me," I told Jeff. He didn't heed my request and instead encouraged me to pull myself out from under the vehicle. That was a much more astute idea and nowhere near as impossible as it had originally seemed.

My way of emotionally coping with coming as close as I ever want to killing myself and thus securing my very own Darwin Award was swift and decisive. As soon as I found what I wanted, I traded in the demonic Subaru and drove off in a new car. My Honda Element had just enough ground clearance to ensure I would never get wedged underneath the car again. As for not running over myself again, that's required the implementation of slightly better judgment that has, thus far, kept me very much alive. For now.

21
Mexican Swine Flu Zombie Apocalypse

My father told me to never go to Mexico, that it was dirty and dangerous and not worth the money saved over other tropical destinations, but I didn't listen. My friends Joe and Cynthia were getting married at a brand new resort in Playa del Carmen in April, and I couldn't book my flight to Cancún fast enough. It was the end of another long ski season when my friend Melissa (yet another coach) and I departed snowy Vermont for the white, sandy beaches of the Caribbean.

Unfortunately, the wedding date didn't match the spring break vacation at my school, so I had to take an extra four-day weekend in order to attend. I found coworkers to cover my supervisory duties as well as my classes for the Friday and Monday I would miss. Joe was the kind of friend whose special day I felt obligated to attend if for no other reason than to demonstrate my solidarity. Although we never worked together, per se, he was the coach of a rival team so we spent innumerable days in each other's company killing time on the side of ski trails while waiting for our respective athletes to race against each other. The bonds that are formed by sharing repeated days of mediocrity and the occasional morning of misery while exposed to the elements over the duration of successive Vermont winters are unbreakable. I was going to Mexico.

My fair-skinned body that had been cloaked from the sun all winter wasn't well suited to the equatorial rays of the lands of Cortés. By that Friday evening in Playa del Carmen, I was nursing quite possibly the worst case of sunburn I have ever experienced. Who knew skin could fry so quickly under a hazy afternoon sky? That's Mexico. Melissa's job as my travel partner instantly transformed from mere companion to official hard-to-reach-spot aloe applicator.

"How bad does it look?" I asked, referencing the middle of my back that was out of view.

"Probably about as bad as it feels," Melissa quipped before breaking into a sinister cackle.

Despite my crispy, charred, well-done appearance, the wedding itself turned out to be absolutely spectacular. Joe and Cynthia could not have been happier exchanging vows on the beach while surrounded by their wedding party, family, and closest friends. It was the way I imagined all weddings should be, without too much fanfare and never inside a stuffy room.

The weather that weekend was the ultimate standard of perfection, and we spent our days lounging poolside while quaffing umbrella-laden drinks garnished with orange wedges. The resort had swim-up bars, and we decided they needed to become a staple in life. At night, we danced and raged like only people in their late-twenties can still do without great consequence. On Saturday afternoon, we took a walk to the nearby nude beach—inhabited only by flabby elders, much to our dismay—and attempted oceanfront yoga, a class in which I only lasted ten minutes before giving up on. I met Joe and Cynthia's friends from all over the United States and abroad, and we spent three days in an isolated paradise with our cell service disconnected and no tethers to the outside world.

It was a refreshing holiday not just from the monotony of my home country but also from the norm that has become modern society. For the first time in years, I didn't find myself constantly reaching for my phone to check email. I was relieved to find myself free of the unfulfilling quest for satisfaction that is hinted at but never delivered by the ping of an electronic device. I went to Mexico for Joe and Cynthia's wedding, but what I found there was anti-modernist bliss.

My first indication that anything could possibly be wrong came just before our departure from the resort when I decided to activate international roaming on my phone to check voicemail. The iPhone vacation was coming to an end. What I wasn't expecting was an overflowing mailbox with more than twenty new messages awaiting response. I didn't even know twenty people had my phone number. My parents had each called multiple times to leave frantic messages, as had some friends and a few of my coworkers. Everyone was asking if I was all right. I had no reason not to be fine while vacationing in Mexico at a gated resort. They hadn't run out of rum, so what could have possibly been wrong? That was when I first learned of the hyperbolic paranoia surrounding the swine flu outbreak of 2009.

Undeterred by alarmist reactions, Melissa and I made our way to the airport to catch our flights home. I had a Tuesday morning class to make back at my school, and she had similar responsibilities at hers. But the sight in Cancún Airport was downright frightening as scores of people lined up wearing surgical masks like Michael Jackson, but they weren't trying to conceal their identities from the paparrazi. My journey home was beginning to resemble any one of a number of end of the world feature films that might be shown during the flight, but this was happening in real life. The sound of coughing on airplanes is disturbing enough, but the sound of people coughing on your airplane during a rare strain influenza outbreak is a whole different kettle of piranhas.

When the plane finally landed in Boston, my roommate Sarah called to tell me I couldn't return to the school. People were worried, there were children and the elderly dying, and I could be a swine flu carrier since I was coming back from Mexico. Whole schools were closing down, and they just couldn't take the risk. I had to stay away, for at least a week, maybe longer, they weren't entirely sure. Nobody really knew, so I would have to wait it out for a while.

Now, I wasn't too bummed about being told I couldn't go to work for a week, because who wouldn't be psyched to extend their weekend into a whole extra week of vacation? But at the time, I lived where I worked, so being banned from work included being banned from going home. It was April in New England, and all I had packed for my trip was a weekend's worth of beach clothes.

I had only checked one small bag on the flight, but all the luggage arriving from Mexico had to undergo additional screening. Maybe they were looking for pigs. I eventually cleared Customs only after promising my first-born child to the agent and swearing on the holy Bible that I had not recently presented any flu-like symptoms.

"I can't even remember the last time I sneezed," I said to the man behind the window. I already felt like a persona non grata in my own country.

It was a crazy night at Boston Logan Airport, and the shuttle service for the economy lot where I had parked my car drove by my terminal stop three times completely full. An equally frustrated couple also trying to get on the shuttle offered to split a cab with me, so I jumped at the opportunity. I was a weary traveler still unsure of my final destination, but getting to my car was the first necessary step. We hopped in a taxi and directed the driver to an off-site parking lot a few miles from the airport.

"Where are you coming home from?" the husband asked me while making polite conversation. Given the hysteria I had already experienced, I was afraid to be honest. If I confessed to where I had really been, would the couple shimmy to the other side of the cab and look upon me with disgust? I thought about the other international cities I saw illuminated on the display board back at the baggage claim, all the flights that had arrived around the same time as mine.

"Reykjavik," I blurted out, fairly certain I had completely butchered the pronunciation of Iceland's capital city.

"Ohhhh, how was that?" the wife asked me, both impressed and intrigued by my fabricated travel location.

"They have really amazing hot springs, kind of like Yellowstone," I answered without missing a beat. I had never even been to Iceland, and I had no idea what I was talking about.

"That sounds like a great trip," the husband said. "We're just coming back from Mexico."

I got to my car, but I still didn't have anywhere to go in it. My brother Mike had rented a lake house in New Hampshire thirty minutes from the airport, so I called to ask if I could stay with him for a few days while waiting out the chaos. He was in the middle of barbecuing for some friends and told me to come on by—the more, the merrier. But as I drove to his house, he phoned back to tell me his wife wasn't comfortable with me staying there. People were dying. No one knew the full extent of the dangers of this illness yet, and I had just flown in direct from the source.

Begrudgingly, I checked into a hotel for the night. After cranking the heat and settling in with my three sundresses and numerous pairs of shorts, I dialed my mother down in New Jersey to see if I could stay at her place, assuming I drove there the following morning. She said it was fine; her daughter was always welcome home no matter what.

Before I could even start the journey to Jersey, another relative caught wind of my plan to seek refuge at my mother's, and he didn't think it was such a good idea. You would have thought I was accused of mass murder given the reaction I received to simply wanting to stay at my childhood home. My elderly grandparents frequently visited my mom, and my mother suffered from multiple sclerosis. The reasoning was that if I stayed at the house and was a carrier of the swine flu, it would spell total disaster. And if my grandparents happened to come over as well, I would kill them all in one fell swoop. Hadn't I realized that people were dropping like flies? Didn't I care enough about my mother and grandparents to just stay away?

After returning home from what was supposed to be nothing more than a long weekend in Mexico for a wedding, I had emerged as the lead actor in a post-apocalyptic blockbuster hit. I imagined my family members telling each other that their loved one was no longer the same person she used to be, you know, before the zombies might have gotten to her. As much as they loved the former me, the possible zombie me wasn't to be trusted. Doors were locked everywhere I turned.

The stress of feeling socially quarantined and the constant fear that perhaps I actually was a carrier of this life-threatening influenza, that maybe I would get sick in a hotel room all by myself and nobody would even know or care, began to take its toll. All I had to wear were skirts and tank tops, and it was fifty degrees outside and pouring raining. I broke down and cried.

That's when my father, the same person who warned me to never go to Mexico and who couldn't say, "I told you so!" fast enough, the man who murdered Santa Claus and assassinated the Tooth Fairy and who ruined a perfectly good powder day by throwing his goggles in the woods, became the only person who pulled through for me in the end. He told me to come stay with him in his condominium. He didn't care if I was sick or if I got him sick or even if I was a zombie who wanted to eat his brain. I finally realized after more than twenty-five years that my father never actually destroyed those fanciful figures from my childhood. He *was* them, all of them, Santa Claus and the Tooth Fairy and the Easter Bunny, wrapped up in the same amazing person. And he was my dad.

Every time I sneezed that week while staying with him, he asked me, "Do you feel okay?" and then chuckled.

I never contracted any flu-like illnesses that spring or the next fall or the next winter. Roughly thirty-six thousand people die every year of the seasonal flu, more than double the victims claimed by the swine flu, officially known as H1N1, in 2009–2010. But for those eight days in April after one long weekend in Mexico, the illness might as well have attacked me. I had nowhere go and a village of angry townsfolk chasing me down with pitchforks and wooden stakes, and I couldn't run very fast in just my flip-flops.

When people discuss these irrational fears, like the inhabitable Earth coming to a sudden end or a *War of the Worlds*-like alien invasion, I no longer feel the urge to panic. Scary movies don't frighten me so much anymore, and I forgave my coworkers and all the family members who told me I wasn't welcome that week. Because of them, I had my dry run of *Independence Day*, that rehearsal for *Night of the Living Dead*, and a firsthand *Outbreak* experience. I don't need an underground bunker in my backyard in order to survive. Having already endured one Mexican swine flu zombie apocalypse, I'm prepared to stare down the next. Life can give me all the lemons it has, because I'm predisposed to telling these ridiculous stories.

Bring it.

CPSIA information can be obtained at www.ICGtesting.com
Printed in the USA
BVOW04*1121270913

332254BV00001B/1/P

9 781457 523380